11/26

# NEW YORK YANKEES TRIVIA TEASERS

D0880001

RICHARD PENNINGTON

TRAILS BOOKS
Madison, Wisconsin

Library of Congress Control Number: 2007923662
ISBN 13: 978-1-931599-83-2
ISBN 10: 1-931599-83-1

Editor: Mark Knickelbine
Designer: Colin Harrington
Photos: National Baseball Hall of Fame Library
Cooperstown, NY

Printed in the United States of America.
12 11 10 09 08 07                    6 5 4 3 2 1

Trails Books, a division of Big Earth Publishing
923 Williamson Street • Madison, WI  53703
(800) 258-5830 • www.trailsbooks.com

# *Table of* CONTENTS

Lou and the Babe.

# Chapter One
# THE ORIGINS

It all began at the dawn of the 20th century with a pair of gentlemen, Frank Farrell and William Devery. The former owned a casino and a number of pool halls, while the latter had recently been forced out of his job as chief of the New York City police department because of blatant corruption. At any rate, Farrell and Devery purchased the Baltimore Orioles, a defunct American League franchise, for $18,000 and moved it to New York in 1903. Even back then, any pro league—and this one was just two years old—that wanted to succeed had to have a team in the country's biggest city. The Brooklyn Superbas (soon to be renamed the Robins and then the Dodgers) and the New York Giants of the National League were already firmly established in New York when the newcomers from the American League arrived.

The team would play in a hastily constructed wooden park at the intersection of 168th Street and Broadway. The site was one of the highest spots in Manhattan. As a result, home field was called Hilltop Park, which is why the team was named the Highlanders. The minimally functional $15,000 park lacked clubhouse facilities in the early years, so players had to dress elsewhere. Seating capacity was 16,000.

The other members of the American League in 1903 were the Washington Senators, St. Louis Browns, Detroit Tigers, Cleveland Naps (Indians), Philadelphia Athletics, Chicago White Sox, and Boston Americans (Red Sox). The Highlanders' first game took place in Washington on April 22; they fell to the Senators, 3-1, but won the next day behind pitcher Harry Howell. The first game at home, like the first two, was against Washington, resulting in a 6-2 win for the Highlanders.

How, and why, did the team come to be called the Yankees? To begin with, we must remember that at the turn of the century, the Civil War was less than 40 years in the past. Some wounds had yet to heal. It was not uncommon for northerners and southerners to call each other "rebels" and "yankees" (or worse). So it wasn't unusual when, as the New York baseball club concluded

1

spring training in Richmond, Virginia, on April 7, 1904, the headline in one of the local newspapers read, "Yankees Will Start Home from South To-Day." After opening day of the 1904 season, the *New York Evening Journal* seemed to have adopted the name: "Yankees Beat Boston." The moniker slowly grew in popularity over the next decade. When the team left Hilltop Park for the Polo Grounds in 1913, the "Highlanders" name had become obsolete, and "Yankees" was used exclusively.

 Let's start with the matter of logos, of which New York has two. Describe them.

 The interlocking "NY" is perhaps the most famous insignia in pro sports. It is a modified version of one created in 1877 by Louis Tiffany to honor the first New York police officer killed in the line of duty. It first appeared on the Highlanders' uniforms in 1909. The other logo consists of "Yankees" written in red script across the seams of a baseball. A bat forming the edge of the "k" is topped with an Uncle Sam–style hat.

 He was a pitcher whose career began in 1891 and did not end until 1914, including five years with New York. As during his time with three other teams, he was a player-manager for the Yankees. Identify him.

 Clark Griffith, also known as "the Old Fox," winner of 236 games. He would own the Washington Senators from 1912 until his death in 1955.

**Q** Wee Willie Keeler was with New York from 1903 to 1909. How small was he?

**A** He stood 5' 4", weighed 140 pounds, and had compiled a 44-game hitting streak in 1897 while playing for the Baltimore Orioles. During that streak (a record broken by Joe DiMaggio 44 years later), a sportswriter asked his secret to batting. Keeler's response: "Keep a clear eye, and hit 'em where they ain't."

**Q** Keeler was the highest paid player in the American League. What was his salary?

**A** $10,000.

**Q** He had played with the Phillies, Reds, and Tigers before being traded to the New York Highlanders in 1903 and was the team's main third baseman for the next seven seasons. He was also a very hot-headed player. Identify him.

**A** Norman Elberfeld, also known as "the Tabasco Kid." He was just 5' 5", but he fought often and well. For example, on September 3, 1906, in a game against the A's, Elberfeld assaulted umpire Silk O'Loughlin and had to be forcibly removed by police. He also seemed to enjoy provoking Ty Cobb.

**Q** More than 25,000 fans were on hand when he threw a wild pitch in the ninth inning of the final game of the 1904 season, allowing the Boston Americans to win the AL pennant. Who was he?

**A** Jack Chesbro. That was an unfortunate ending to an otherwise astonishingly successful year for "Happy Jack." He started 51 games and finished 48 of them (plus four relief appearances) for a record of 41-12. He pitched 454 $^2/_3$ innings that year.

**Q** Name the catcher who failed to grab Chesbro's pitch in that final game of 1904.

**A** John "Red" Kleinow, who some fans faulted although the pitch sailed high over his head.

**Q** How did Chesbro come by his nickname?

**A** It was actually an ironic reference to his dour disposition. Chesbro was said to have served as a janitor in a psychiatric ward during his younger days.

**Q** Right around the turn of the century, pitcher Al Orth's career was going down. Then he was traded to the Highlanders, and what happened?

**A** He learned the spitball from Chesbro and proceeded to lead the AL with 27 wins in 1906.

**Q** How successful were the New York Highlanders?

**A** Not very. They came in second in the American League in 1904, 1906, and 1910, but they were usually in the middle of the pack, and sometimes in the cellar (1908 and 1912).

**Q** Who was Hal Chase?

**A** He was regarded by Babe Ruth, Walter Johnson, and others as the best first baseman yet to play the game. "Prince Hal" was with the Highlanders from 1905 to 1913, with the White Sox from 1913 to 1914, with the Reds from 1916 to 1918, and with the Giants in 1919. An excellent hitter and a wizard with the glove, he nevertheless personified the corruption of major league baseball in the pre–Black Sox era. Allegations of gambling and corruption surrounded Chase wherever he went. He may not have helped fix the 1919 World Series, but he knew about it and made a tidy $40,000 betting on the Reds. In 1921, commissioner Kennesaw Mountain Landis banned Chase from the game for life.

**Q** If Chase was such a good defensive player, why did he lead the league in errors for first basemen seven times?

**A** An excellent question.

**Q** Frank Delahanty played first base, second base, and outfield for New York in 1905, 1906, and 1908. But what made him unusual?

**A** He was one of five Delahanty brothers to make it to the big leagues, along with Ed (a Hall of Famer, primarily with the Phillies), Jim, Joe, and Tom.

**Q** Branch Rickey, of course, is best known for bringing Jackie Robinson into the major leagues in 1947, but he was also a player. What did his career consist of?

**A** Rickey was a catcher and outfielder with the Browns in 1905 and 1906 and with the Yankees in 1907. In 120 games, he batted .239.

**Q** He had attended Penn State before embarking on a baseball career with the New York Highlanders/Yankees from 1908 to 1915. Who was he?

**A** William "Birdie" Cree, who peaked in 1911 when he batted .348, hit 22 triples, and stole 48 bases.

**Q** What franchise record does Jack Warhop hold?

**A** Most hit batters in a season—he plunked 26 in 1909. He hit 114 in an eight-year career, which is still a franchise record.

**Q** This pitcher was a master of the doctored ball, which was entirely legal at the time. His best year was 1910, when he went 26-6, had an ERA of 1.65, and struck out 209 batters. Who was he?

**A** Russ Ford.

**Q** This man, another spitballer, had worked in the Pennsylvania coal mines and as a blacksmith before being signed by the Highlanders in 1909. Who was he?

**A** Jack Quinn. His career did not end until 1933 when he was with the Cincinnati Reds, his eighth team. At that time, Quinn was 50 years old; he finished with 247 victories and 218 losses.

**Q** Who was New York's primary catcher in the early 1910s?

**A** Jeff Sweeney. In 1914, he stole 19 bases—which still stands as a team record for catchers.

**Q** From 1910 to 1918, he was the ace of an otherwise sorry pitching staff. He had a nasty spitball and could pinch-hit, too. Identify him.

**A** Ray "Slim" Caldwell, who went on to help the Indians win the 1920 World Series.

**Q** This Vermont native started 166 games for the Highlanders/Yankees from 1910 to 1917. Who was he?

**A** Ray "Chic" Fisher, a member of the Cincinnati Reds team that won the tainted 1919 World Series.

**Q** What is the worst record of any team in the history of the franchise?

**A** The 1912 New York Highlanders won 50 and lost 102, finishing 55 games behind the Red Sox.

**Q** When did pinstripes first appear on the Highlanders' uniforms?

**A** In the 1912 season.

**Q** So the Yankees had New York all to themselves in what seasons?

**A** From 1958 to 1961.

**Q** Was polo ever played at the Polo Grounds?

**A** During earlier incarnations of the stadium (the first was in 1883), yes, but not since the last one was built in 1913.

**Q** When have the Yankees shared quarters with other teams?

**A** It has happened thrice. First, for two months in 1911, when the bathtub-shaped Polo Grounds was being rebuilt after a fire, the Giants played at Hilltop Park. The Giants returned the favor by letting the Yankees use the Polo Grounds from 1913 to 1922. And in 1974–1975, during renovation of Yankee Stadium, they were at the Mets' Shea Stadium in Queens. The Yankees, Giants, and Mets cooperated to this extent; there was never such an overlap with the Brooklyn Dodgers, however. The Giants and Dodgers high-tailed it to San Francisco and Los Angeles, respectively, in 1958. At that time, the Dodgers' Ebbets Field met the wrecking ball, but the Polo Grounds, a bonanza of oddities and idiosyncrasies, had a second baseball life when the expansion New York Mets used it in 1962 and 1963. It was razed soon thereafter.

The value of the franchise had appreciated considerably by 1915, when it was bought for $1.25 million. Name the two men who purchased it.

Jacob Ruppert and Tillinghast L'Hommedieu Huston, both of whom went by the honorary title of "Colonel." Seven years later, Col. Ruppert would buy out Col. Huston for $1.5 million.

What were the highlights of Jacob Ruppert's career?

He inherited a brewery from his father and served four terms in Congress. He owned the Yankees for 25 years (from 1915 until shortly before his death in 1940), turning the previously moribund franchise into a powerhouse. Always willing to wheel and deal, he brought in Ed Barrow as GM and managers like Miller Huggins and Joe McCarthy. Yankee Stadium was his baby, too.

A plaque on the center-field wall of Yankee Stadium was dedicated after Ruppert's death. How did it characterize the Colonel?

"Gentleman, American, sportsman, through whose vision and courage this imposing edifice, destined to become the home of champions, was erected and dedicated to the American game of baseball."

**Q** Was Ruppert part of the Tammany Hall political machine?

**A** So it is said, and that did not hurt when he began planning the construction of Yankee Stadium.

**Q** He is the only shortstop to ever lead his team in home runs, and he did it twice. Who was he?

**A** Roger Peckinpaugh. However, he had just three homers (in 1914) and five (in 1915) in those pre-Ruth, "dead-ball seasons" before the cork-core ball made home runs more frequent. Peckinpaugh was later American League MVP with the Senators and manager of the Indians.

**Q** Fred Maisel was quite a thief on the basepaths. What did he do for the Yankees back in the 1910s?

**A** In 1914, this Maryland native stole 74 bases, which stood as a team record until Rickey Henderson broke it in 1985. In one game in 1915, he stole second, third, and home. And he stole home 14 times in his career. No wonder they called him "Flash."

**Q** Which of the High brothers (Andy, Charlie, or Hugh) played for the Yankees?

**A** Hugh. He was a regular in New York's outfield from 1915 to 1917.

**Q** Frank "Home Run" Baker didn't hit many home runs, did he?

**A** In a 13-year career, the first seven with the Athletics, he hit 96 homers. But we must keep in mind the era in which he played. In the context of the times, he was quite prolific, leading the American League in 1911 (11), 1912 (10), 1913 (12), and 1914 (9). Philly won the World Series three times with Baker patrolling third base. He sat out the 1915 season in a contract dispute and then spent six years with New York, although his productivity declined somewhat.

**Q** He tried and failed in brief stints with the Yankees in 1915 and 1918, but a decade in the minors had taught him how to pitch—which he did with Brooklyn for 11 seasons. Name this one who got away.

**A** Clarence "Dazzy" Vance, who won most of his 197 games for the Dodgers. National League MVP in 1924 with a record of 28-6, he soon became the best-paid pitcher in baseball. Vance created a lot of memories at Ebbets Field.

**Q** What Yankees pitcher was the first to throw a no-hitter?

**A** George Mogridge, who did it against the Boston Red Sox at Fenway Park on April 24, 1917.

**Q** Who was Ping Bodie?

**A** His real name was Francesco Stephano Pezzolo, and he was one of the most feared sluggers of his time. Obtained from the Philadelphia A's in 1918, Bodie roomed with Babe Ruth—or as he so often put it, he roomed with Ruth's suitcase. He has long been regarded as the first person of Italian descent to play in the major leagues. And he did inspire many who followed, such as the DiMaggio brothers, Tony Lazzeri, and Frank Crosetti.

**Q** This man played football at the University of Alabama before getting into pro baseball for a 13-year career. Who was he?

**A** Del Pratt, a fine second baseman who batted .292. He played with the Yankees from 1918 to 1920, but he gained notoriety for something that happened in 1917 when he was with the St. Louis Browns. The team owner, Phil Ball, accused some of his players, including Pratt, of loafing in order to be traded. Pratt was offended, so he sued Ball for slander. Needless to say, he was soon an ex-Brown.

**Q** What North Dakota native played catcher for the Yankees from 1918 to 1920?

**A** James "Truck" Hannah. But when Wally Schang arrived, it was time for Truck to hit the road.

**Q** He played baseball, football, and basketball at the University of Illinois and earned a degree in civil engineering. He was good enough to make the Yankees' 1919 team, but in 12 games he came to bat 22 times and got just two hits. Who was he, and what did he do next?

**A** George Halas, and he helped found the Chicago Bears and the National Football League.

**Q** He played three seasons for the Yankees (1919, 1920, and 1922) and one for the Red Sox, primarily as a left-handed pitcher. Then a sore arm caused him to fall to the minors, where he spent four years learning how to hit and play the outfield. Name this person.

**A** Lefty O'Doul, who came back to the majors with a bang. His best season was 1929, when he batted .398, had 254 hits and 32 home runs, drove in 122 runs, and scored 152 himself. O'Doul later served as manager of the San Francisco Seals of the Pacific Coast League, helping to develop Joe DiMaggio. As if that were not enough, he was baseball's goodwill ambassador to Japan, both before and after World War II.

A fan's view from the right-centerfield bleachers of Yankee Stadium.

## Chapter Two
# BABE RUTH AND HIS BIG NEW HOUSE

The Yankees were rolling along, but they were perhaps the least popular of New York's three major league teams. If they envied anyone, though, it was not the Giants or Robins but the Boston Red Sox, winners of five World Series championships. And since 1914, the Sox had employed a pitcher-turned-hitter named George Herman "Babe" Ruth. His skills seemed to grow with every year.

In 1915, Ruth was 18-8, batted .315, and hit his first four big-league home runs. The Red Sox beat the Phillies in the Series, although Ruth did not pitch and was 0-for-1 at the plate. In 1916, he was the best pitcher in the American League, going 23-12 with a 1.75 ERA and nine shutouts. Boston beat Brooklyn in the World Series, and Ruth pitched a 14-inning complete-game victory. He was exceptional again in 1917—24 wins and 13 losses, although the Chicago White Sox won the pennant. Ruth batted .325. The next season, pitching less (13-7) and batting more, he tied Tilly Walker of the A's for the home run title with 11. At this early point, Ruth was arguably the top player in the game, and the best was yet to come. Boston beat the Chicago Cubs for the crown in 1918, and Ruth extended his streak of consecutive scoreless World Series innings to 29 $2/3$.

In 1919, his final year with the BoSox, Ruth had further curtailed his pitching and moved to the outfield. His numbers were impressive—29 home runs (a new record), a .322 batting average, and 114 RBI. Ruth's feats were the talk of baseball fans in every city. But he was as troublesome as he was talented. There were countless indiscretions, late-night partying and boozing, curfew violations, and escalating contract demands. The *enfant terrible* ended up getting sold to the New York Yankees prior to the 1920 season. He may have had second thoughts about the team he was going to, however. In Ruth's six major league seasons, the Yankees had been true also-rans, finishing from 7 $1/2$ to as many as 30 games back between 1914 and 1919.

In retrospect, it would become clear to all that this transaction sent the two franchises in opposite directions—New York as a perennial winner and Boston as the very opposite. Every season from 1920 to 1934 (Ruth's time as a Yankee), the Red Sox finished between 20 $1/2$ and 59 games behind.

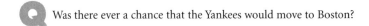

**Q** Was there ever a chance that the Yankees would move to Boston?

**A** As a matter of fact, yes. Red Sox owner Harry Frazee had bought his team on credit and was having legal problems. One of many discussions held between Frazee and New York's owners (and AL president Ban Johnson) was the possibility of moving the Yankees franchise to New England, merging with or even supplanting the Red Sox.

**Q** What did Frazee's financial problems lead him to do?

**A** Trade or sell some very good players—including pitchers Waite Hoyt, Carl Mays, and Herb Pennock, catcher Wally Schang, shortstop Everett Scott, third baseman Joe Dugan, and, of course, Babe Ruth—to the Yanks. No fewer than 11 ex-Sox players were on the 1923 New York team that won the World Series.

**Q** What did the Red Sox get in return for Babe Ruth on January 3, 1920?

**A** Money—$125,000 and a $350,000 loan against the mortgage on Fenway Park.

**Q** What were Frazee's words to the press two days later?

**A** "It would be impossible to start next season with Ruth and have a smooth-working machine. Ruth had become simply impossible, and the Boston club could no longer put up with his eccentricities. I think the Yankees are taking a gamble. While Ruth is undoubtedly the greatest hitter the game has ever seen, he is likewise one of the most selfish and inconsiderate men ever to have put on a baseball uniform."

**Q** What about the oft-told story of Frazee using the funds from the Ruth deal to finance his Broadway musical comedy *No, No, Nanette?*

**A** No, no, it is untrue. Frazee did not produce that play until 1925.

**Q** Carl Mays was a Kentucky native who threw underhanded, was another spitballer, feuded with Ty Cobb, was considered a troublemaker—he was rumored to have thrown games—and was the first pitcher to win 20 games for three teams (the Red Sox, Yankees, and Reds). But he is best known for what tragic incident?

**A** On August 16, 1920, Mays was on the Yankee Stadium mound, facing Ray Chapman of the Cleveland Indians. Chapman was crowding the plate when Mays came in with his fast-rising submarine ball. It hit Chapman flush on the temple, and he died the next day. Ray Chapman remains the only major league player to have died as a result of an on-field incident.

**Q** He was once described as a pitcher with a million dollars worth of talent and just 25 cents worth of enthusiasm. Who was he, and why were such unkind words said about him?

**A** We refer to former Texas A&M football star Rip Collins, who had a 25-13 record for the Yanks in 1920 and 1921. The real pleasures in his life were hunting and fishing in the off-season, and boozy parties during the season. Perhaps this is why he was soon traded to Boston.

**Q** Who generally batted fifth in the fabled "Murderer's Row?"

**A** Bob Meusel. This 6' 3" left fielder enjoyed an 11-year career (10 with New York, one with the Cincinnati Reds) and had a .309 average, 368 doubles, 94 triples, 156 home runs, and 1,067 RBI. His brother, Irish, played for the crosstown Giants, and they faced each other in four World Series. Meusel was considered the goat of the 1926 Series because he dropped a fly ball that allowed the St. Louis Cardinals to win a game and thus the Series.

**Q** What did Meusel do on June 13, 1924?

**A** He precipitated one of the worst brawls in the history of the sport. In Detroit, Meusel was hit by a pitch thrown by the Tigers' Bert Cole. He took his bat to the mound where players from both teams engaged in a fight that included many fans who rushed onto the field. When the police were unable to break it up after 30 minutes, umpire Billy Evans ruled that the Tigers had forfeited the game. Meusel, Cole, and Ruth were fined and suspended.

**Q** Name the manager who guided the Yanks to their first six AL pennants and three World Series titles between 1918 and 1929.

**A** Miller Huggins.

**Q** What about Huggins as a player?

**A** He was a switch-hitting second baseman for the Reds (1904–1909) and Cardinals (1910–1916). Just 5' 6", Huggins batted in a crouch that made for a tiny strike zone, which allowed him to lead the NL in walks four times. His managing career began in 1913, even while he was playing for St. Louis.

**Q** What was the first Subway Series?

**A** It came in 1921, when the Yankees and Giants played eight games (all at the Polo Grounds), with John McGraw's team winning five. Waite Hoyt won two games and Babe Ruth hit the first of his 15 World Series home runs.

**Q** He was known as "the Schoolboy Wonder" because he signed his first pro contract at age 15 and the "Merry Mortician" because he worked as a funeral director in the off-season. Who was he?

**A** Pitcher Waite Hoyt, who had a 21-year career. His best seasons (1921–1929) were with the Yankees. He went 22-7 with the 1927 team.

**Q** This fine catcher already had two World Series titles (with the A's and Red Sox) to his credit before joining the Yankees in 1921. Who was he?

**A** Wally Schang. He spent five years in New York and may be considered the first in a string of great catchers—along with Bill Dickey, Yogi Berra, Elston Howard, and Thurman Munson. Schang won one ring with the Yankees (1923) and another with the A's (1930, as a backup for Mickey Cochrane) before hanging it up.

**Q** Who served as New York's general manager and then president from 1921 to 1945, and was largely responsible for all that success?

**A** Ed Barrow. He had been manager of the Tigers (1903–1904) and Red Sox (1918–1920) before joining the Yankees. He used canny trades, a deep farm system, and outright purchases of top players to build the dynasty. He is also supposed to have discovered future Hall of Fame shortstop Honus Wagner in 1892 and to have turned Babe Ruth from a pitcher into a hitter. The latter claim is highly dubious, since Ruth had been good with the bat even when he was at the reform school in Baltimore.

**Q** What happened in Yankees history on July 26, 1922?

**A** There were two fights in the dugout—first between Bob Meusel and Wally Schang, then Babe Ruth and Wally Pipp went at it. After that, they whacked the St. Louis Browns, 11-6.

**Q** He was known as "Jumping Joe" because he often took unauthorized leaves from the team. Who was he?

**A** Joe Dugan, New York's third baseman from 1922 to 1928. His best year may have been 1923, when he hit .283 and scored 111 runs for the champs. Dugan was the starting third baseman for the '27 Yankees, although his skills were beginning to erode by then. He also spent time with the A's, Red Sox, Braves, and Tigers.

**Q** One of the first pitchers to master the forkball, he was 26-7 for New York in 1922. Identify this native of Brainerd, Minnesota.

**A** "Bullet" Joe Bush. Since Bush had a career batting average of .253, he was sometimes put in right field on non-pitching days.

**Q** How did Babe Ruth do in the 1922 World Series?

**A** Not too well. He got two hits in 17 at-bats for a .118 average. The Giants swept the Yankees in four games (with one tie).

**Q** What prompted the building of Yankee Stadium?

**A** Babe Ruth had joined the team in 1920 and had an utterly spectacular season: a .376 batting average, 54 home runs, and an AL pennant. The Bambino brought out fans like crazy, as attendance more than doubled (from 619,000 in 1919 to 1.3 million in 1920). The Giants, owners of the Polo Grounds, were none too happy to see their co-tenants outdrawing them and issued an eviction notice. Within months, the Yankees announced that they had purchased 10 acres of land in the west Bronx for a triple-decked structure (eventually built with two decks) that would far surpass the Polo Grounds just across the Harlem River.

**Q** Who designed Yankee Stadium, who built it, and what did it cost?

**A** The Osborne Engineering Company of Cleveland, the White Construction Company of New York, and $2.5 million.

**Q** Construction on Yankee Stadium began on May 5, 1922, and it was ready for the season opener in 1923. What happened that day?

**A** A crowd of 74,200 was on hand to witness New York's 4-1 defeat of Boston. Ruth hit the stadium's first home run. Before that, however, John Philip Sousa and the Seventh Regiment Band led both clubs to the flagpole in deep center field, where the American flag and the Yanks' 1922 pennant were raised.

**Q** How much of an attendance bump did the Yankees get from building this huge stadium?

**A** None at first. In fact, average attendance in 1923 (13,251) was slightly below what it had been in the last year at the Polo Grounds (13,326).

**Q** A young man named Lou Gehrig was attracting attention for his play at Columbia University. What Yankees scout signed him?

**A** Paul Krichell signed Gehrig for $1,500 for the remainder of the 1923 season and also offered a $2,000 bonus.

**Q** He was the man of iron before Gehrig came along, appearing in 1,307 straight games with the Red Sox and Yankees. Who was this fine shortstop?

**A** Everett Scott. He led AL shortstops in fielding percentage for eight seasons in a row and batted .318 in the 1923 World Series.

**Q** In the '23 Series (the first played in Yankee Stadium), it was the Giants and Yankees for the third straight time. Did Miller Huggins's boys finally come through with a title?

**A** Yes, they did. Second baseman Aaron Ward hit .417. Ruth had three homers, drew eight walks, and scored eight runs. Herb Pennock won the final game.

**Q** He came over from the Red Sox in 1922 and a year later was the hero of the Yankees' first World Series title. Identify him.

**A** "Sad" Sam Jones, who went 21-8 in 1923 and saved the final game against the Giants in the Series. He had a 22-year career with six American League clubs, but that was his most memorable season.

**Q** Who was the star for the Giants in that Series?

**A** Casey Stengel, who hit two home runs and robbed Ruth of one in deep center field. He was then promptly traded to the Boston Braves.

**Q** This left-handed pitcher spent time with the A's and Red Sox before joining the Yanks, helping them win titles in 1923, 1927, and 1932. Identify him.

**A** Herb Pennock, a native of Kennett Square, Pennsylvania. He finished with 240 wins and a 3.60 ERA, and his record in World Series play was 5-0. Pennock would serve as general manager of the Phillies from 1944 to 1948.

**Q** When did Lou Gehrig's streak of 2,130 consecutive games begin?

**A** On June 1, 1925, when he pinch-hit for Pee Wee Wanninger. It ended on May 2, 1939, when the Yankees and Tigers met in Detroit.

**Q** Wally Pipp is often remembered as simply the man who, the day after Gehrig pinch-hit for Wanninger, relinquished his starting first base job to him. But he actually had a long and productive career. What were the highlights of that career?

**A** He played for 15 years (11 with the Yanks), had a .281 average, and participated in three World Series. Pipp, who scouted Gehrig at Columbia and urged the team to sign him, did all he could to help Gehrig master the nuances of first base. And, to set the record straight, Pipp did not just sit out a game with a headache, as has so often been stated. The team was in a slump, and Miller Huggins benched several veterans in an effort to shake things up.

**Q** What did Pipp do in the 1923 World Series?

**A** Due to injuries, he was taped from ankle to hip on both legs. But he appeared in all six games, had five hits and two RBI, and played errorless ball.

**Q** When the '25 Yanks finished in seventh place in the AL, attendance at home games plummeted. How bad was it?

**A** They averaged 8,826 fans per game in a stadium that had an official seating capacity of 58,000. Attendance would drop below 9,000 again in 1935 and 1943.

**Q** Let's discuss the formative years of the Sultan of Swat. What happened to Babe Ruth in 1904?

**A** His parents placed him in St. Mary's Industrial School for Boys for his "incorrigible" behavior—such as skipping school, drinking, chewing tobacco, and fighting. He spent almost his entire youth at St. Mary's, where he developed into a fabulous baseball player with the encouragement of a man known as Brother Matthias.

**Q** What did Japanese soldiers scream at their American counterparts during World War II?

**A** "To hell with Babe Ruth!"

**Q** Ruth had set a new record for home runs in a season in 1919, while still with Boston. Who held the record before?

**A** Ned Williamson of the Chicago White Stockings hit 27 in 1884, but he played home games in a minuscule park. So that record may be viewed with skepticism.

**Q** Ruth did not have a great season in 1925. What happened?

**A** In spring training, he fell victim to his own indulgences of eating and drinking (it was known as "the bellyache heard around the world"). He was diagnosed with an intestinal abscess, which required surgery. Ruth missed much of the season and served out a suspension by manager Miller Huggins for insubordination—not a rare occurrence.

**Q** So what were his stats in 1925?

**A** Ruth appeared in just 98 games, and the Yankees finished the season 69-85. He batted .290, hit 25 home runs, and drove in 66 runs.

**Q** What were Babe Ruth's proportions?

**A** He stood 6' 2" and weighed 215 pounds.

**Q** How often did Ruth pitch with the Yanks?

**A** He was on the mound one game in 1920, two in 1921, and one each in 1930 and 1933, for a total of five games. Ruth's overall record as a pitcher: He won 94 games and lost 46, had an ERA of 2.28, and struck out 488 batters.

**Q** What was Ruth's last hurrah?

**A** He was playing with the Boston Braves on May 25, 1935, when he hit three homers in Pittsburgh. One week later, batting just .181, he announced he was quitting at the same time the Braves said he was released. Ruth held 56 major league records at the time.

**Q** What legendary manager played for the Yankees in the late 1920s?

**A** Leo Durocher. A feisty infielder of whom Babe Ruth was not fond, Durocher scratched out a 15-year career mostly with the Reds, Cardinals, and Giants. But it was as a manager that Leo the Lip won his fame. He was with the Brooklyn Dodgers in 1947 when Jackie Robinson came to camp. Durocher also nurtured Willie Mays with the New York Giants, who won the 1954 World Series. Before he was through, Durocher (who also spent time with the Cubs and Astros) was fifth among major league baseball managers with 2,008 victories.

**Q** In 1925, the Yankees purchased the contract of a player with the San Francisco Seals who was coming off one of the greatest minor league seasons ever. Who was he and what did he do in '25?

**A** We speak of second baseman Tony Lazzeri, who hit 60 home runs and drove in 222 runs that year. He went on to have a long (1926–1937) career with New York. Lazzeri had a well-deserved reputation as a clutch player, and he was another home run threat along with Ruth and Gehrig. At the end, he played with the Cubs, Dodgers, and Giants.

**Q** Lazzeri was also handy with his fists. How did he explain it?

**A** "It was fight or get licked, and I never got licked."

**Q** Identify the longtime Yank who lost his job to Lazzeri in 1926 and was soon traded to the White Sox.

**A** Aaron Ward.

**Q** This master of the spitball and other junk pitches won 37 games for New York in 1926 and 1927. Who was he?

**A** Urban Shocker. He had been with the Yanks in 1916 and 1917 before being traded to St. Louis. Manager Miller Huggins soon came to regret the trade because Shocker pitched brilliantly with the woeful Browns. And to make matters worse, he seemed to get Babe Ruth out with ease. So he was reacquired in a move that paid big dividends.

**Q** The Yankees were up three games to two in the 1926 World Series coming back to the Bronx. Surely they could close out the Cardinals, right?

**A** Wrong. Grover Cleveland Alexander won Game 6, celebrated long into the night, and came back to pitch 2 ⅓ innings of relief to help St. Louis upset New York. The series ended when Ruth made an ill-advised attempt to steal second base. Nevertheless, Ruth would never play in another losing World Series game—the Yanks swept in 1927, 1928, and 1932.

**Q** From 1926 to 1929, he and Tony Lazzeri were the Yankees' double-play combination. Who was he?

**A** Shortstop Mark Koenig.

**Q** Yes, but what did Koenig do in the 1926 Series?

**A** He committed four errors, one of which let the Cardinals win Game 7. In the '27 World Series, however, he did much better, getting nine hits in 18 at-bats as the Yankees whacked Pittsburgh. Koenig later played in the Fall Classic with the Cubs (1932) and Giants (1934).

**Q** What seven members of the 1927 Yankees are in the Hall of Fame?

**A** Babe Ruth, Lou Gehrig, Herb Pennock, Miller Huggins, Waite Hoyt, Earle Combs, and Tony Lazzeri.

**Q** Who else was on that team?

**A** Julie Wera, Mike Gazella, Pat Collins, Benny Bengough, Ray Morehart, Myles Thomas, Cedric Hurst, Urban Shocker, Joe Dugan, Mark Koenig, Dutch Ruether, Johnny Grabowski, George Pipgras, Wilcy Moore, Don Miller, Bob Meusel, Bob Shawkey, Joe Giard, Walter Beall, and Ben Paschal. The coaches were Charlie O'Leary and Art Fletcher, the trainer was Doc Wood, and the mascot was Eddie Bennett.

**Q** Who was the keen-eyed center fielder and leadoff man on the 1927 Yankees team, batting .356 that year?

**A** Earle Combs, a.k.a. "the Kentucky Colonel." In his 12-year career, he had 670 walks and led the league in triples three times.

**Q** And what did Combs's manager, Miller Huggins, have to say about him?

**A** "If you had nine Combses on your ball club, you could go to bed every night and sleep like a baby." Combs, it should be noted, was a refined man who did not indulge in tobacco or strong drink.

**Q** Who was on the mound when Ruth hit his 60th home run on the final day of the 1927 season?

**A** Tom Zachary of the Washington Senators. He and Ruth were later teammates for three years. Zachary won one game in the 1928 World Series, and in '29 he went 12-0 and had an ERA of 2.48. As for Ruth's last homer in 1927: In the clubhouse after the game, an elated Ruth shouted, "Sixty, count 'em, sixty! Let's see some son of a bitch top that!"

**Q** Gehrig won the first of his two MVP awards in 1927. What were his numbers?

**A** They were big: a batting average of .373, 172 RBI, and 47 homers.

**Q** How did Gehrig fare in the 1932 World Series against Chicago?

**A** He whipsawed the Cubs' pitching staff with a .529 average, scored eight runs, had nine RBI, and hit three home runs.

**Q** How consistent was Gehrig?

**A** Consider these stats: he had more than 100 RBI 14 years in a row, more than 20 doubles 15 years in a row, and more than 27 dingers 13 years in a row.

**Q** What player has the most grand slams in baseball history?

**A** Lou Gehrig. The Iron Horse hit 23 in his career, which lasted from 1923 to 1939.

**Q** Who had the unenviable task of facing the Yankees in the 1927 World Series?

**A** Pittsburgh. Some NL supporters even predicted that the Pirates would win, although New York had taken the AL pennant by 19 games, Ruth had his 60 home runs, Gehrig was league MVP, and Huggins had a very strong pitching staff. Before Game 1, Ruth and his mates put on a demoralizing show, blasting ball after ball into the Forbes Field bleachers.

**Q** New York swept that Series, 4-0. Who was on the mound for the Yanks in the final game?

**A** Rookie Wilcy Moore. He would never again approach the 19 games he won that year.

**Q** What happened after the Bucs had been dispatched?

**A** Ruth, Gehrig, and others went on a very lucrative 22-game barnstorming tour.

**Q** The '27 Yankees, who batted .307 and outscored their opponents by 376 runs, were said to be a team for the ages, the greatest in baseball history. Is it true?

**A** Up to that point, probably so. But it would be another 20 years before Jackie Robinson broke the color barrier, and then came players from such lands as Cuba, the Dominican Republic, Venezuela, Japan, Taiwan, and Korea. So it is enough to say that the 1927 Yankees were the best of the pre-integration era.

**Q** What was the first major enlargement of Yankee Stadium?

**A** The left field stands were expanded to three decks prior to the 1928 season. The same thing was done to the right field stands in 1937, at which time the center field fence was brought in from 490 to 461 feet.

**Q** Who did the Yankees beat in the 1928 Series?

**A** St. Louis. Ruth and Gehrig abused Cardinals pitchers unmercifully, batting a combined .593, hitting seven homers, and driving in 13 runs.

**Q** In spite of that two-man show, New York's pitchers did something unusual against the Cards. What was it?

**A** Waite Hoyt had two complete games, and George Pipgras and Tom Zachary had one each. It was the last time a team would use just three pitchers in a World Series.

**Q** Pipgras had a league-high 24 wins in 1928 and pitched in 300 innings. What did he do after an arm injury abruptly ended his playing career?

**A** He became an umpire for a decade, working the 1940 All-Star Game and the 1944 World Series.

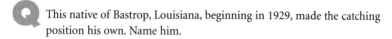

**Q** This native of Bastrop, Louisiana, beginning in 1929, made the catching position his own. Name him.

**A** Bill Dickey. Possessed of a strong arm, an ability to handle pitchers, and a relentlessly competitive nature, he is still one of the all-time greats behind the plate. He hit over .300 every year but one between 1929 and 1939, peaking in 1936 with a .362—the highest single-season average ever for a catcher. Dickey was a player-manager in 1946, retired, and then came back as a coach so he could pass on his vast experience to Yogi Berra.

**Q** He started playing major league baseball in the late 1920s and didn't stop until the early 1950s. Who was this man of steel?

**A** Pitcher Louis "Bobo" Newsom. In his one season with the Yanks (1947), he had a 7-5 record and a 2.80 ERA.

**Q** Who served as the Yankees' manager for one year (1930) after the untimely death of Miller Huggins?

**A** Bob Shawkey.

**Q** What was Shawkey's background as a player?

**A** He had a 15-year career as a pitcher—two and a half with the A's and the rest with New York. He won 20 games four times and was there when the Yankees became the greatest team in baseball. Huggins picked him to pitch the first game at Yankee Stadium in 1923. When the stadium was reopened after a two-year renovation in 1976, he threw out the first ball. Fired after guiding the team to a third-place finish in 1930, Shawkey later managed in the Pittsburgh and Detroit farm systems, and coached at Dartmouth.

**Q** This outfielder was with the Yankees in the early 1930s and would later win a National League batting crown. Identify him.

**A** Fred "Dixie" Walker. His father had pitched for the Senators, his uncle was an outfielder for the Browns, and his brother (Harry "the Hat") played for four teams and managed the Cardinals, Pirates, and Astros.

**Q** Walker was with the Dodgers in 1947 when Jackie Robinson arrived. What was Walker's response?

**A** The Georgia native was not at all happy, requesting that club president Branch Rickey trade him. His wish was not granted until 1948, when he went to Pittsburgh. It should be noted, however, that Walker's view of Robinson and integration evolved over the years.

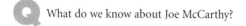

**Q** What do we know about Joe McCarthy?

**A** He had a 15-year minor league career but never made it to the bigs. His first managing job was with the Chicago Cubs, who he led to the 1929 NL title. He joined the Bronx Bombers in 1931. McCarthy's strict but fair style of managing worked: New York won the World Series in 1932 and four straight from 1936 to 1939. The Yanks won three more AL crowns (1941–1943) before he resigned, due in part to a conflict with GM Larry McPhail. He also spent three years with the Boston Red Sox. McCarthy had his detractors, but historians today regard him as one of the best managers baseball has seen.

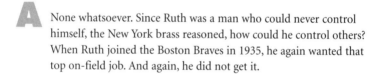

**Q** Babe Ruth campaigned openly for the manager's job that was given to Shawkey and then to McCarthy. Was there any chance of him getting it?

**A** None whatsoever. Since Ruth was a man who could never control himself, the New York brass reasoned, how could he control others? When Ruth joined the Boston Braves in 1935, he again wanted that top on-field job. And again, he did not get it.

**Q** This southpaw pitcher was known for saying "I'd rather be lucky than good," but he was both—going 189-101 for the Yanks from 1930 to 1942. Who was he?

**A** Lefty Gomez. He won pitching's "triple crown" (wins, ERA, and strike-outs) twice and had a 6-0 record in World Series play. Gomez was the winning pitcher in the first All-Star Game (in 1933) and drove in the first run of the game, although he was a notoriously bad hitter.

**Q** How high does Gomez rank in the Yankees' pitching pantheon?

**A** He is third in wins, seventh in winning percentage, fourth in strikeouts, fourth in shutouts, and second in complete games.

**Q** On what date did Babe Ruth become the first major leaguer to hit 600 career home runs?

**A** August 21, 1931, when the Yankees defeated the St. Louis Browns, 11-7.

**Q** After 11 years with the Indians (for whom he played 1,103 straight games), Joe Sewell joined New York and held down the third base spot from 1931 to 1933. What was so unique about Sewell as a hitter?

**A** He was just about impossible to strike out. In 7,132 at-bats, Sewell whiffed just 114 times. He was a little guy, just 5' 6", but he swung a 40-ounce bat. Sewell's career batting average of .312 indicates that he was more than just a contact hitter.

**Q** Since he lost a whopping 47 games for the Red Sox in 1928 and 1929, he would seem to be a most unlikely candidate for the Hall of Fame. But he did in fact get enshrined four decades later. Identify this person.

**A** Red Ruffing. First of all, that lousy record with Boston is deceiving since he got very little offensive support. Traded to New York in mid-1930 and buoyed by the offensive production of Babe Ruth, Lou Gehrig, and others, Ruffing was an ace. He appeared in seven World Series, where he had a 7-2 record. He was also an excellent hitter, with 36 homers and a .269 batting average.

**Q** Who was New York's third baseman for most of the 1930s?

**A** Red Rolfe. His offensive peak came in 1939 when he amassed 213 hits, scored 139 runs, and batted .329. During Rolfe's career, the Yankees won 16 World Series games and lost just three. He was later the athletic director at Dartmouth, baseball and basketball coach at Yale, and manager of the Detroit Tigers from 1949 to 1952.

**Q** Gehrig performed what feat on June 3, 1932?

**A** He became the first player to hit four home runs in a game. It was at Philadelphia, and the Yankees beat the Athletics, 20-13. He would have hit a fifth in the ninth inning but Al Simmons snatched it at the wall.

**Q** This 6' 4", 295-pound pitcher was a surprisingly agile fielder. He was with the Yankees from 1932 to 1936 before moving on to the Reds and Giants. Who was he?

**A** Walter "Jumbo" Brown.

**Q** This outfielder was a big contributor to New York's success in the early 1930s. In the 1932 World Series, he batted .294 with six RBI as the Yankees swept the Chicago Cubs. Who was he?

**A** Ben Chapman, who later played with several teams in both leagues.

**Q** What legendary moment occurred during the '32 World Series?

**A** In Game 3, the score was tied, 4-4, in the fifth inning when Ruth came to the plate. There had been considerable bad blood between the two teams from the start. Whether Ruth "called" his home run or whether he pointed to center field (or merely back at pitcher Charlie Root) before launching the ball there—these things have long been debated. His home run, which quieted a raucous crowd at Wrigley Field, turned out to be the last Ruth ever hit in a World Series.

**Q** That 1932 title was most satisfying to whom?

**A** Manager Joe McCarthy, who had been with the Cubs from 1926 to 1930.

**Q** This New Jersey native was 27 when he made his major league debut with the Yankees in 1933, and what a debut it was: He shut out Washington (by a score of 16-0) and went 4-for-4 at the plate. Who was he?

**A** Russ "the Sheriff" Van Atta.

**Q** What happened in a game against Detroit in the summer of 1936?

**A** Journeyman Myril Hoag was playing center field and rookie Joe DiMaggio was in right when they went for a fly ball in the gap, collided, and both were knocked unconscious. The Tigers' Goose Goslin got an inside-the-park home run on the play.

**Q** This bespectacled Yale grad won 39 games for the Yanks between 1934 and 1936, but he jumped the team twice and was finally released. Who was he?

**A** Johnny Broaca.

The 1927 New York Yankees, one of the greatest teams ever. Lou Gehrig is
on the back row, far left; Babe Ruth is four down from him; manager
Miller Huggins is fifth from the left in the middle of the second row.

## Chapter Three
# AN ERA ENDS, A NEW ONE BEGINS

Even the greatest of the great—and that surely describes Babe Ruth—must step aside at some point. The Yankees' front office had been making plans for life after Ruth as early as 1930. They reduced his salary, started looking for replacements, and failed to show the kind of respect or at least gratitude that such a rare player should merit. At any rate, Ruth was soon on his way to a short stint with the Boston Braves and then life outside of the game. Lou Gehrig, with whom he had feuded for years, carried on for most of the 1930s before falling victim to a disease (amyotrophic lateral sclerosis) that now bears his name.

California golden boy Joe DiMaggio would quickly earn superstar status of his own. Pitchers like Lefty Gomez and Red Ruffing helped to ensure more titles—four straight from 1936 to 1939. And even with things turned upside down during the war years, New York won more often than not. General manager Ed Barrow and his successor, George Weiss, had built a farm system (with as many as 20 teams) that virtually guaranteed an unending supply of fine baseball players. The best of those eventually got to the Bronx, but who knows how many others just gave up after a while.

It was Weiss, by the way, who made the surprising choice of Casey Stengel to be the team's new manager in 1949. During Stengel's 12-season tenure in the Yankees' dugout, rarely did the team not challenge for or win the World Series.

**Q** On November 21, 1934, the Yankees paid $50,000 for the contract of what minor league player?

**A** Joe DiMaggio, a shortstop/center fielder for the San Francisco Seals.

**Q** He grew up in the same San Francisco neighborhood that produced DiMaggio and was the Yankees' main shortstop from 1932 to 1948. Name this man, whose calling cards were consistency and durability.

**A** Frankie "the Crow" Crosetti. He was a master of the hidden-ball trick and still holds the team record for most times hit by a pitch—114. After retiring, Crosetti served as third base coach for 20 years, taking part in 15 more World Series.

**Q** Who succeeded Babe Ruth in right field for the Yankees?

**A** George "Twinkletoes" Selkirk. He did not match Ruth's charisma and power-hitting ability—none could—but during the next eight seasons, Selkirk batted over .300 five times, twice had more than 100 RBI, played on five title teams (1936, 1937, 1938, 1939, and 1941), and was an American League All-Star in 1936 and 1939. He was no stiff.

**Q** How did the Yankee Stadium fans take to the new right fielder at first?

**A** They booed him unmercifully, but he persevered and was a big part of Joe McCarthy's ongoing dynasty. Selkirk later served as general manager of the Washington Senators.

**Q** This native of Oakland, California, won one game per World Series from 1936 to 1939. Who was he?

**A** Monte Pearson, who threw a no-hitter against his old team, the Indians, in 1937.

**Q** He was a part-time infielder with the Yankees from 1934 to 1937 before moving to the St. Louis Browns, for whom he played a more substantial role. Who was he?

**A** Don "Jeep" Heffner, who would have a short and unsuccessful stint as manager of the Cincinnati Reds in 1966.

**Q** No less an authority than Hank Aaron has called him the greatest player he ever saw. Who was he?

**A** Joseph Paul "Joe" DiMaggio. At 6' 2" and 198 pounds, he was a master of just about every facet of the game. He was smooth, with a big swing and quick reflexes. DiMaggio ran the bases well, and he covered lots of ground in center field. When he got to the Yankees' training camp in 1936, he was not at all worried about making it—not after batting .398 with the San Francisco Seals of the Pacific Coast League.

**Q** Were the Yankee's veterans at all doubtful or threatened by this fabulous newcomer from the West?

**A** Some were, but they were soon won over. DiMaggio's talents fit in quite well with Gehrig, Dickey, Lazzeri, Rolfe, et al. The adoring New York press couldn't get enough of him.

**Q** Joltin' Joe had two baseball-playing brothers. Who were they?

**A** Both were outfielders like Joe. Vince spent 10 years with the Braves, Reds, Pirates, Phillies, and Giants. Dom played 11 years with the Red Sox.

**Q** What transpired at Philadelphia's Shibe Park on May 24, 1936?

**A** The Yankees enjoyed a 25-2 laugher over the Athletics. Tony Lazzeri had two grand slams and a third homer, Joe DiMaggio had three hits, including a homer, and even Frankie Crosetti went deep. Ben Chapman had five of New York's 16 walks. Monte Pearson was the winning pitcher.

**Q** What are the most memorable facts about Jake Powell?

**A** First, the good part. He went 10-for-22 and scored eight runs in the 1936 World Series. But this reckless outfielder once instigated a conflict with Hank Greenberg of the Detroit Tigers that left Greenberg with a broken wrist; Powell's unbridled anti-Semitism may have played a part. On May 30, 1938, in a 10-0 victory over the Red Sox witnessed by a Yankee Stadium record crowd of 83,533, Powell was hit by a pitch thrown by Boston's Archie McCain. He rushed the mound but was intercepted by Joe Cronin. The men fought for two minutes before being pulled apart and ejected from the game. But they then met under the stands and continued their brawl until umpire Cal Hubbard (recently retired from pro football) put an end to it himself. Both were fined and suspended for 10 days. Not long after that, Powell gave an interview full of racist remarks and threats—and was once again suspended. He had been out of baseball for three years when he was taken into a Washington, D.C., police station on a bad-check charge. There, he pulled out a pistol and killed himself.

**Q** He played football, basketball, and baseball at the University of Georgia, spent 11 years (1937–1947) in pinstripes, and had a .717 winning record. Who was this fine pitcher?

**A** Spud Chandler. He was American League MVP—still the only Yankees pitcher to be so named—in 1943 with a 20-4 record, 1.64 ERA, and two complete-game wins over the St. Louis Cardinals in the World Series.

**Q** Once again shuttling between Yankee Stadium and the Polo Grounds, it was McCarthy's Yankees versus Bill Terry's Giants in the 1937 World Series. Who prevailed?

**A** Despite the best efforts of pitcher Carl Hubbell, the Giants had little chance, winning but one game. Gehrig hit his 10th and final World Series home run, and second baseman Tony Lazzeri had a triple in the deciding game. It was New York's sixth championship in the past 15 years.

**Q** Who served as the Brooklyn Dodgers' first base coach in 1938?

**A** Babe Ruth, who was still angling for a job as a manager.

**Q** The Chicago Cubs were back in the World Series in 1938 after a six-year hiatus. Did they do any better against the Yankees than in 1932?

**A** Not at all—they got the broom both times. Pitchers Red Ruffing, Lefty Gomez, and Monte Pearson were too much for the Cubbies.

**Q** There was a familiar face on the Cubs' roster in that World Series. To whom did it belong?

**A** Second baseman Tony Lazzeri, who had helped the Yanks win five championships. Facing his old team in the Series, Lazzeri got no sweet payback, however. He was hitless in two at-bats, and Chicago was squashed.

**Q** Who was Lazzeri's replacement with the Yanks?

**A** Joe "Flash" Gordon, and a worthy replacement he was. In his first year in the majors, Gordon had 25 home runs, 97 RBI, and scored 83 runs. Known for his acrobatic defense, he meshed well with his other infield mates—Rolfe at third, Crosetti at short, and Gehrig at first.

**Q** And how did Gordon do in the '38 World Series?

**A** Splendidly. He batted .400, had six RBI, and won Game 3 by himself with a solo homer in the fifth inning and a two-run single in the sixth.

**Q** Recount Gordon's 1942 season.

**A** He put together a 29-game hitting streak, batted .322, and had 173 hits. For that, he won the American League MVP award.

**Q** What did Gordon do after New York traded him in 1947?

**A** He had four solid seasons with the Indians, during which time he helped ease the way for Larry Doby, the American League's first black player. Gordon managed briefly in Cleveland, Detroit, and Kansas City—both with the A's and later with the Royals.

**Q** What was Lou Gehrig's last game as a Yankee?

**A** The date was June 12, 1939. In an exhibition game against the Kansas City Blues, New York's AA farm team, the Iron Horse, played just three innings. Batting eighth, he ground out weakly to second base in his only time up.

**Q** Ho-hum. Another year, another World Series sweep for the Yanks. Who was the victim in 1939?

**A** The Cincinnati Reds, making their first appearance since the 1919 Series. Game 4 at Crosley Field went into extra innings, but the Reds committed three errors and gave away their last chance.

**Q** What's the sad postscript to that '39 World Series?

**A** Gehrig had played the first eight games of the season before benching himself on May 2. He gave his heart-wrenching "luckiest man on the face of the earth" speech at Yankee Stadium on June 4 and traveled with the team the rest of the season, and to Cincinnati and back after the World Series. But the heirs of the late Col. Ruppert (who owned the team until 1945) told Gehrig that he should find a job because there was nothing for him in the organization. Gehrig's soon-to-be widow, Eleanor, remembered that for years.

**Q** Who did Gehrig mention by name in that famous speech?

**A** Ruppert, Barrow, Huggins, and McCarthy. Whether by design or not, he did not refer to Ruth.

**Q** And what job did Gehrig hold in his remaining time before dying?

**A** He was a parole commissioner in New York City.

**Q** This tall lefthander was one of New York's first bonus babies, signing in 1940 for $10,000. He had a 72-40 record in 11 years of service (plus time spent with the Browns, White Sox, and Senators). Who was he?

**A** Tommy Byrne, who threw a complete-game win against the Dodgers in Game 2 of the 1955 World Series. He had control problems, leading the AL in batters hit five times and walks three times. Byrne was also a fine hitter, with 14 home runs and 98 RBI to his credit. He later served as the mayor of Wake Forest, North Carolina.

**Q** How long did Mel Allen serve as "the voice of the Yankees?

**A** From 1939 to 1964 (except for World War II, when he was in the U.S. Army), he broadcast every game New York played. Loquacious and possessed of a distinctive southern accent—he was an Alabama native—Allen was one of the most prominent members of his profession. He had signature catchphrases but managed never to annoy the listener. After his firing in 1964, for reasons that were never fully explained, he worked with the Milwaukee Braves and Cleveland Indians. Allen was back with the Yankees' on-air family a decade later and stayed active with syndicated shows and other media until shortly before his death in 1996. To some people, he embodied the spirit of the national pastime.

**Q** He, Joe DiMaggio, and Tommy Henrich formed one of the best outfields in baseball during the 1940s. Who was he?

**A** Charlie Keller. Known as "King Kong" although he stood but 5' 10", Keller had an agricultural degree from the University of Maryland. His most productive season may have been 1941, when he hit .298 with 33 homers, 122 RBI, 24 doubles, and 15 triples.

**Q** When did Joe DiMaggio's 56-game hitting streak begin?

**A** On May 15, 1941, with a single off Edgar Smith of the Chicago White Sox. It did not end until July 17 when he went 0-for-3 in the Yanks' 4-3 defeat of Cleveland. The Indians' third baseman, Ken Keltner, twice robbed DiMaggio of hits with fine fielding plays. Let's also recall that he proceeded to get at least one hit in each of his next 16 games.

**Q** What was the controversy about the 1941 American League MVP award?

**A** DiMaggio won it, but Ted Williams of the Red Sox (with his .406 batting average) had very strong credentials as well. One voter stubbornly refused to put Williams on his top-ten list.

**Q** This 5' 6", 150-pound shortstop was the sparkplug for the Yankees' engine from 1941 to 1956, minus the war years. Identify him.

**A** Phil Rizzuto, also known as "Scooter." A master of small-ball skills like bunting, stealing bases, sacrificing, and the hit-and-run, he was MVP of the American League in 1950. Rizzuto scored five runs in the '51 Fall Classic and got an MVP award there, too. He was also a very good defensive player, once handling 238 straight chances without an error—a record for shortstops. After his retirement (a *forced* retirement, actually, as most of them are), Rizzuto began a 40-year career as a broadcaster.

**Q** After Rizzuto graduated from high school in Brooklyn, he attended tryouts with the Yankees, Giants, and Dodgers. The Yankees must have been underwhelmed when they first signed Rizzuto. What kind of bonus did he get?

**A** $75.

**Q** What insult did Casey Stengel, then manager of the Dodgers, lob at Rizzuto during that time?

**A** He suggested Rizzuto work as a shoeshine boy. Stengel, to his credit, became one of the converted, comparing Rizzuto with the great Honus Wagner.

**Q** The 1941 World Series was four games to one over the Brooklyn Dodgers, but it was closer than it looked. What memorable play happened in the ninth inning of Game 4 at Ebbets Field?

**A** Dodgers pitcher Hugh Casey threw a breaking curveball (or was it a spitball?) past Tommy Henrich for an apparent strikeout, but catcher Mickey Owens could not handle it. The Yankees proceeded to score four runs over the demoralized Dodgers.

**Q** He kept opposing hitters off balance with a wide array of deliveries and was a mainstay of manager Joe McCarthy's 1941, 1942, and 1943 pennant winners. Who was he?

**A** Ernest "Tiny" (he was 6' 2" and weighed 215 pounds) Bonham, who spent six years in New York and three more in Pittsburgh. He threw a four-hitter against the Dodgers in Game 5 of the 1941 World Series, clinching the title for New York.

**Q** The war years had begun, so everything in the sports world was askew. (For example, the World Series was scheduled for a 3-4 format due to travel restrictions.) Nevertheless, the Yankees won another pennant in 1942. Who did they beat in the World Series this time?

**A** Surprise—they lost! Their foes were the defending champion St. Louis Cardinals, with 106 National League victories to their credit. Billy Southworth's club took it in five games.

**Q** Right-handed pitcher Hank Borowy had gone 46-25 for the Yanks in his first three seasons and was 10-5 and an All-Star in 1945. Then what inexplicably happened?

**A** He was put on waivers, hooked up with the Cubs, and went 11-2 the rest of the way, helping them reach the World Series. Joe McCarthy was so upset with this decision that he quit in 1946. His teams had won 1,460 games.

**Q** What is most memorable about George "Snuffy" Stirnweiss?

**A** A native of New York, he went down to the University of North Carolina and became a star football player for the Tar Heels. As a second baseman, he played 10 years in the major leagues with the Yankees, Browns, and Indians. Stirnweiss was a key contributor in New York's winning the 1947 World Series. He led the AL in stolen bases twice and in batting once.

**Q** He attended Fordham University, spent 12 seasons with the Yankees (minus the war years, as with so many of that generation), and was a star out of the bullpen—indeed, one of his nicknames was "the Fireman." Who was he?

**A** Johnny Murphy, who pitched in eight World Series games. He won two and lost none, saved four, and had an ERA of 1.10. He was later a front-office man with the Red Sox and Mets.

**Q** This New Jersey native signed with New York in 1937 for a piddling $100 bonus and then spent six years working his way up through the minor leagues. He started every game of the 1943 season at shortstop and did so well that he was fourth in MVP voting. Identify him.

**A** Billy Johnson. He played on four championship clubs (1943, 1947, 1949, and 1950) before being traded to the Cardinals.

**Q** The 1943 World Series was a reprise of the Yankees and Cardinals. Did the Yankees bring the trophy back to New York?

**A** Yes, they did. With third baseman Billy Johnson and catcher Bill Dickey leading the offensive attack, Spud Chandler taking two complete-game victories on the mound, and McCarthy in control in the dugout, it was a surprisingly easy 4-1 Series.

**Q** This left-hander, nicknamed "Old Reliable," was a key figure for New York in three World Series—1941, 1947, and 1949. Name him.

**A** Tommy Henrich. In the latter series, he had a walkoff homer against the Dodgers' Don Newcombe in Game 1 and scored twice in Game 5 as the Yanks took another championship. He later coached with the Yankees, Giants, and Tigers.

**Q** He'd already won the NL batting title three times with the Pirates, but his skills had been in decline for five years when the Yankees picked him up in 1944. Who was he?

**A** Paul "Big Poison" Waner. Famous for his ability to play while hung over, Waner had given up drinking well before he got to New York.

**Q** His father (Ray) and uncle (Roy) had played in the majors in the 1920s. He was New York's primary third baseman in 1944 and 1945. To whom do we refer?

**A** Oscar Grimes. He hit well enough to make the All-Star team but was an atrocious fielder, committing 55 errors in those two seasons.

**Q** This first baseman attended Villanova and was one of the Yankees' better players in the World War II era. Who was he?

**A** Nick Etten, who hit 54 home runs from 1943 to 1945. Etten was part of the '43 World Series champs and was on the AL All-Star team in 1945.

**Q** When did the franchise next change hands?

**A** Prior to the 1945 season, Dan Topping, Del Webb, and Larry McPhail bought it for $2.8 million from the estate of Col. Ruppert. McPhail was chosen as president and GM. They, in turn, sold it to CBS two decades later for $13 million. In 1973, the network sold it to a group headed by Cleveland shipping magnate George Steinbrenner. Interestingly enough, in nine years the price had gone *down* to $10 million. Since then, the value of the franchise has gone up, up, up to more than $1 billion.

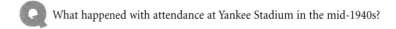

**Q** What happened with attendance at Yankee Stadium in the mid-1940s?

**A** The Yanks averaged 11,603 per game in 1945, but it jumped to 29,422 the next season.

**Q** Babe Ruth was obviously sick by the mid-1940s. How was he honored?

**A** On April 27, 1946, Babe Ruth Day was celebrated in ballparks throughout the major leagues. On June 13 of that year, his number (3) was retired and he made his final appearance at Yankee Stadium. By August 16, 1948, he was dead of throat cancer at age 53.

**Q** How did DiMaggio do upon returning from the Navy in 1946?

**A** Things were not as easy as before, and he had more injuries, but DiMaggio was a uniquely great player. He led the Yankees to titles in four of his last six years.

**Q** What did the Yanks do in 1946 in terms of travel accommodations?

**A** They became the first major league team to fly to away games.

**Q** A most unusual player joined the Yankees in 1946—a third baseman who would pursue a medical degree in his off-seasons. Who was he?

**A** Bobby Brown. He had attended Stanford and UCLA, and started at Tulane medical school even as World War II was going on. The enterprising Brown usually missed part of spring training and went straight to New Orleans until he graduated in 1950, specializing in cardiology. Brown, who once helped rescue a Coast Guard officer after a plane crash, could also play ball, although he seemed to save his best for the 17 World Series games in which he took part. His postseason average of .439 is the highest among players with at least 40 at-bats. Brown served as president of the American League from 1984 to 1994.

**Q** In 1947, he was the winner of the All-Star Game, had a 14-5 record, and won Games 1 and 5 of the World Series. Who was he?

**A** Frank "Spec" Shea, whose promising career was cut short by a neck injury.

**Q** He stood 6' 1", weighed 205 pounds, and was a menacing presence on the mound. He went 111-48 from 1948 to 1953 and never missed an assignment. Who was this fastballer?

**A** Vic Raschi. He was also a fine hitter; in a game against Detroit in 1953, he had seven RBI, then a record for pitchers.

**Q** What other "achievement" is Raschi known for?

**A** Pitching for the St. Louis Cardinals at Sportsman's Park on August 4, 1953, he gave up the first of Hank Aaron's 755 home runs.

**Q** What happened in franchise history on May 26, 1946?

**A** It was the first night game ever at Yankee Stadium—a 2-1 loss to Washington before 49,917 fans.

**Q** The Yankees won the 1947 World Series, four games to three, over their neighbors, the Brooklyn Dodgers. Who was New York's manager?

**A** Bucky Harris, who had won a title 23 years earlier with the Washington Senators.

**Q** The two most memorable plays in that Series came at the hands of "Dem Bums." Recall them.

**A** In Game 4, the Yankees' Bill Bevens had thrown 8 $^2/_3$ innings of no-hit ball, but then he walked the first two batters and gave up a long, right-field hit to Cookie Lavagetto. And just like that, Bevens lost his no-hitter and the game. Then, in Game 6, more than 74,000 fans at Yankee Stadium saw Joe DiMaggio smash a ball to deep center field, but Al Gionfriddo made what some called the greatest catch in baseball history, snuffing a New York rally. Oddly enough, it was the last game in the careers of Bevens, Lavagetto, and Gionfriddo.

**Q** He started two games at catcher (ahead of Yogi Berra) for the Yanks in the 1947 World Series but soon moved on, playing primarily for the White Sox for many years. Who was he?

**A** Sherman Lollar. When he retired in 1963, he had the highest career fielding average for a catcher (.992) in major league history.

**Q** Name the Pennsylvanian with the lively fastball who struggled as a starter until Harris moved him to the bullpen, where he thrived.

**A** Joe Page. He entered Game 7 of the 1947 World Series and shut down the Dodgers for the last five innings, giving up just one hit.

**Q** He had spent four years with the White Sox. Then, from 1948 to 1955 he was the third of the "big three" on the Yankees' pitching staff. Who was he?

**A** Eddie Lopat. While Allie Reynolds and Vic Raschi were fastballers, he used slower "junk" pitches to frustrate enemy hitters. Thus, one of Lopat's nicknames—"the Junk Man." His best year was 1953, when he went 16-4. Lopat went on to serve as manager of the Kansas City A's for two years in the early 1960s.

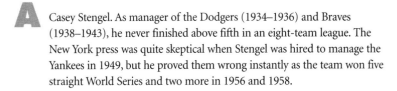 This hard-nosed outfielder was a native of Kansas City and had a rather undistinguished 14-year major league career (with the Dodgers, Pirates, Phillies, Giants, and Braves). But he did hit two home runs in the 1923 World Series. Identify him.

Casey Stengel. As manager of the Dodgers (1934–1936) and Braves (1938–1943), he never finished above fifth in an eight-team league. The New York press was quite skeptical when Stengel was hired to manage the Yankees in 1949, but he proved them wrong instantly as the team won five straight World Series and two more in 1956 and 1958.

Stengel's Yankees were a juggernaut. What did "the Old Perfessor" do to help the cause?

He was one of the game's sharpest tacticians, platooning brilliantly, using pinch-hitters, and cultivating young talent as well as dealing with veterans' egos. Stengel's sarcasm and wit have sometimes overshadowed just what a fine manager he was.

In 1949, this man joined the Yankees' farm system and spent four years there, never getting close to the bigs. He did, however, become a scout and executive for several organizations, including the Pirates, Royals, Orioles, and Yankees. Identify this man.

You must be speaking of Syd Thrift.

**Q** Was there really serious discussion of swapping Joe DiMaggio and Ted Williams?

**A** In fact, there was. In 1949, Boston and New York had such a plan in the works but it fell apart because Sox owner Tom Yawkey wanted Yogi Berra thrown in. Yankees president and GM Larry McPhail said no go.

**Q** This outfielder, a native of Akron, Ohio, played a big part in New York's string of titles from 1949 to 1953. But Stengel often platooned him with Hank Sauer, which made for some loud and profane dugout discussions. Who was he?

**A** Gene Woodling. In 26 World Series games with the Yankees, he batted .318. Almost a decade after their heyday in pinstripes, Stengel and Woodling were reunited with the expansion New York Mets.

**Q** What first baseman/outfielder was batting .340 in Pittsburgh when New York acquired him in late 1950 as insurance?

**A** Johnny Hopp, whose 14-year major league résumé would include two titles with the Cardinals and two with the Yanks.

Mickey Mantle awaits his turn at bat.

## Chapter Four
# MORE WINNING—
# AND THEN A SWOON

One was a funny-looking, funny-talking catcher from St. Louis, one was a cocky pitcher from right there in the big city, and the third was a speedy and powerful kid from Oklahoma. Yogi Berra, Whitey Ford, and Mickey Mantle surely had help from teammates in the next two decades, but these were the cornerstones. Fans and the media seemed in accord on the matter.

The Yankees won with brutal efficiency: five straight championships from 1949 to 1953, and the only American League team that gave them much trouble was the Cleveland Indians. New York faced its crosstown rival, the Brooklyn Dodgers, in the World Series seven times in 16 years, winning all but once. Soon the Dodgers and Giants would be winging it out west, leaving New York all to the Yankees, at least until the Mets were born.

Then Casey Stengel was fired and GM George Weiss saw the writing on the wall, quitting before the same thing happened to him. The Yankees' pipeline of talent began to dry up. Mantle and Roger Maris had that unforgettable pursuit of Babe Ruth's home run record in 1961, and the team was in the World Series five straight years but lost three times, to the Pirates, Dodgers, and Cardinals. By the mid-1960s, things had really degenerated. The 1921–1964 dynasty that had brought 29 pennants to Gotham was over, at least for a decade.

**Q** Who was "the Chairman of the Board?"

**A** Whitey Ford. This New York City native joined the Yankees in 1950 and was considered the junior partner of Allie Reynolds, Vic Raschi, and Eddie Lopat, but not for long. Despite losing two full seasons to service in the Korean War, Ford quickly became the undisputed ace of the staff. He lacked an overpowering fastball, but he had pinpoint control and the knack of staying calm and in command during high-pressure games. In a 16-year career (all with New York), he was never better than in 1961 when he went 25-4, won the Cy Young Award, and was World Series MVP.

**Q** New York's opponents in the 1950 World Series were the Philadelphia Phillies, called "the whiz kids" due to their youth and hustle. Given that the franchise was making its first appearance in the Series in 35 years, how did the young men do?

**A** They tried very hard but were no match for Stengel's Yankees. It was a sweep in which the New York pitching staff gave up just three earned runs.

**Q** He is on the short list of the greatest catchers ever, was MVP of the American League three times, and is one of only six managers to lead both AL and NL teams to the World Series. Who is he?

**A** Lawrence Peter "Yogi" Berra of St. Louis, Missouri. He played 19 years with the Yankees, appeared in 14 World Series, and won 10 championships. It has been said that only Bill Russell of the Boston Celtics was a more prolific winner in pro sports.

**Q** What else is Berra known for?

**A** He quit school in eighth grade, so he tended to fracture the English language in ways that were comical yet provocative. Entire books have been written about Berra's verbal missteps, but here are a few: "I never said half the things I really said," "It's like déjà vu all over again," "Nobody goes there anymore—it's too crowded," and perhaps most famously, "It ain't over 'til it's over."

**Q** Name the scout who found Mickey Mantle.

**A** In 1948, Yankees scout Tom Greenwade traveled to Kansas, to watch a semipro game. As often happens, he was there to see another player. When Mantle hit two monstrous home runs (one from the right side, one from the left), Greenwade wanted to sign him on the spot, but he had to wait a year for Mantle to graduate from high school in Commerce, Oklahoma.

**Q** What did Mantle sign for?

**A** $400 to play the rest of the 1949 season in a Class D league, with a $1,100 bonus. It was one of the biggest steals in baseball history. Greenwade, for his part, called Mantle the best prospect he had ever seen.

**Q** Mantle played his entire major league career (1951–1968) for the Yankees. What did he have to show for those 18 seasons?

**A** He won three American League MVP awards, was on the All-Star team 16 times, and played on 12 pennant winners—including seven World Series winners.

**Q** Mickey Mantle was known for hitting some of the longest home runs in major league history. Name two of them.

**A** On April 17, 1953, at Griffith Stadium in Washington, he faced the Senators' Chuck Stobbs and hit a homer that had Mel Allen flabbergasted; it was alleged to have traveled 565 feet. And on September 10, 1960, he hit a moon-shot that cleared the right-field roof at Briggs Stadium in Detroit, finally stopping in a lumber yard across Trumbull Avenue. If we can believe those who measured it, the ball traveled 643 feet.

**Q** Mantle was primarily a center fielder for New York, but he did play a few games at other positions. What were they?

**A** He started at right field in 1951 (DiMaggio's last year) before moving to center. Mantle was at third base for one game in 1952, shortstop for one game in 1953, shortstop for four games and second base for one game in 1954, and shortstop for two games in 1955. At the end, in 1967 and 1968, he was a full-time first baseman.

**Q** Recount Mantle's 1956 season.

**A** He was just 24 years old when he won the Triple Crown and the MVP. He batted .353, with 52 homers and 130 RBI in a superb all-around season. Mantle also scored 132 runs, had a .705 slugging percentage, and stole 10 bases in 11 tries.

**Q** In 1961, Mantle became the highest paid player in major league baseball. How much was he making?

**A** $75,000, which was $5,000 less than Babe Ruth had earned 30 years earlier.

**Q** Mantle's popularity followed an interesting trajectory. What was it?

**A** Some New York fans and sportswriters were down on him initially because he was not the suave and urbane DiMaggio. He also had a military exemption due to a childhood bout with osteomyelitis, and some people took offense at that. But by the early 1960s, the Yankees were indisputably "Mickey's team." He was a wildly popular icon of the sport from there on.

**Q** What World Series records does Mantle still hold?

**A** Most home runs (18), RBI (40), runs (42), walks (43), extra-base hits (26), and total bases (123).

**Q** How many walk-off home runs did Mantle hit in his career?

**A** 12.

**Q** What injuries did Mantle have to deal with?

**A** Chronic bone infections, a broken foot, knee problems, shoulder separations, and torn hamstrings were the main ones. And if the truth is told, Mantle's alcoholism did not help matters. Of course, the same is true for Babe Ruth and countless other baseball heroes.

**Q** This man had flown 57 combat missions in World War II before embarking on his career as a pro baseball player. He got to the Yanks in 1949 and had a fine rookie year at the plate and at second base. Who was he?

**A** Jerry Coleman. Soon, though, he was back doing military service—in Korea. That wiped out much of the 1952 and 1953 seasons. Coleman was a bench player most of the rest of his career, but he finished with a flourish by hitting .364 in the 1957 World Series versus Milwaukee. He went on to become an announcer, both for the Yankees and the San Diego Padres—a team he managed in 1980.

**Q** This player's fame mainly derived from years of success with the St. Louis Cardinals and New York Giants, but he did contribute a lot to the Yankees' string of success in the early 1950s. Who was he?

**A** Johnny Mize. Obtained in a trade late in the 1949 season, he was a first baseman who moved with feline grace and carried a big stick. He is the only major leaguer to hit 50 home runs in a season while striking out fewer than 50 times; in 1947, when he was with the Giants, he had 51 homers and just 42 strikeouts. Mize had a very high on-base percentage, and thus in light of sabermetric analysis, his accomplishments are valued even more today than when he played. Like Joe DiMaggio, Ted Williams, and Hank Greenberg, he lost three years from the heart of his baseball career due to military service in World War II. Otherwise, Mize would have considerably more than 359 home runs.

**Q** The Yankees gave up on this young pitcher much too soon. He made two relief appearances in 1950 before being shipped off to the Boston Braves. Name him.

**A** Lew Burdette. He authored a no-hitter in 1960 and finished his 18-year career with a 203-144 record. He also helped the Braves (by then in Milwaukee) beat his ex-mates in the 1957 World Series.

**Q** Another rookie of sorts debuted at Yankee Stadium in 1950. Despite a very long career, he has yet to play a game. Who is he?

**A** Bob Sheppard. A speech teacher in the New York City school district and a public address announcer for sports events at St. John's University (his alma mater), he became the Yankees' announcer that year. He began working home games for the New York Giants football team in '56. Sheppard retired from that gig in 2005 but is still behind the microphone for the Yanks.

**Q** Who was the first person to play in both the Rose Bowl and the World Series?

**A** Jackie Jensen. First, his football achievements: Jensen was a star halfback at the University of California in 1948. The Bears lost that season's Rose Bowl contest to Northwestern. But Jensen also excelled at baseball, leading Cal to the first College World Series championship. After one year of minor league ball, he was with the Yankees in the 1950 Series against the Phillies. With the arrival of Mickey Mantle, Jensen's value dropped and so he was traded to Washington and from there to Boston. He was American League MVP with the Sox in 1958.

**Q** Infielder Gil McDougald was 1951 AL rookie of the year, five times an All-Star, and played in 53 World Series games. But he is best remembered for what tragic incident?

**A** On May 7, 1957, he was batting against Herb Score of the Cleveland Indians. A line drive hit Score in the eye, causing him to miss the rest of the season and most of 1958. Score valiantly tried to regain his touch (he had won 36 games in his first two seasons, 1955 and 1956), but he could not. McDougald, who anguished over the matter for years, was later the baseball coach at Fordham University.

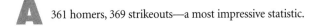

**Q** When Joe DiMaggio retired after the 1951 season, what was his career home-run-to-strikeout ratio?

**A** 361 homers, 369 strikeouts—a most impressive statistic.

**Q** What New York pitcher threw two no-hitters in the 1951 season?

**A** Allie Reynolds, who did it against Cleveland and Boston. He is one of those players who, had he spent most of his career with another franchise, might have gotten more recognition. In a 13-year career, he won 182 games and was equally adept as a starter or reliever. Reynolds really shone in postseason games (which then meant only those in the World Series— no league championship series, no division championship series, no wild card games), with a 7-2 record, four saves, and a 2.79 ERA.

**Q** After Reynolds had his pair of no-hitters, more than three decades would pass before another Yankee threw one. Identify this pitcher.

**A** Dave Righetti, who did it on July 4, 1983, against the Red Sox.

**Q** Who was Johnny Sain?

**A** A fine pitcher with the Boston Braves (achieving poetic immortality with teammate Warren Spahn—"Spahn and Sain, and pray for rain"). He became a reliever with the Yankees at the end of the 1951 season. Sain was later a well-regarded but opinionated pitching coach with a number of teams. He irked the owners and GMs for whom he worked by often urging his pitchers not to fear "climbing the golden stairs" to ask for more money.

**Q** The 1951 World Series (won in six games over the New York Giants) was the end for one great center fielder and the beginning for two more. Name them.

**A** Joe DiMaggio and the youngsters, Mickey Mantle and Willie Mays. None played major roles in the Series, however. Hank Bauer's three-run triple in the sixth inning clinched the final game.

**Q** He was the Yankees' primary first baseman from 1950 through 1957. Who was this native of Scranton, Pennsylvania?

**A** Joe Collins, whose home run won Game 2 of the 1951 Series. He hit another in Game 1 of the '53 Series, and two in the opener of the '55 Series.

**Q** Yes, the Yankees won it all again in 1952, but they had quite a World Series with the Dodgers. What happened?

**A** It came down to Game 7 in Brooklyn. Mickey Mantle's homer in the sixth inning put New York up to stay, Billy Martin made a big catch at second base, and Bob Kuzava came in to save the game—as he had done in the '51 finale.

**Q** Who played third base for New York from 1952 to 1959 and led the league in triples in 1955?

**A** Andy Carey.

**Q** The Brooklyn Dodgers went 105-49 to win the NL flag and had to be considered the favorites in the 1953 World Series, even though the Yankees had won it the previous four years. Who prevailed?

**A** To the dismay of Yankees-haters throughout the land, New York won in six games. Billy Martin had 12 hits and was the Series MVP, and a 25-year-old Vin Scully joined Mel Allen in the TV announcers' booth.

**Q** This man was born dirt-poor in East St. Louis, Illinois, joined the Marines shortly after Pearl Harbor, and won two Bronze Stars and a couple of Purple Hearts in 32 months of combat in the Pacific Theater. As a result, his baseball career was delayed—he didn't make it to the majors until he was 26. Identify him.

**A** Hank Bauer. He patrolled right field in Yankee Stadium for most of the 1950s and was the manager of the Baltimore Orioles when they won the 1966 World Series.

**Q** He was a substitute for Yogi Berra in 1953 and 1954, and Elston Howard would be signed in 1955, rendering him expendable. Who was he?

**A** Gus Triandos, who was traded to the Orioles before the 1955 season. He had a fine career, too—playing more than 1,200 games with them, the Phillies, and the Astros. Triandos was behind the plate in 1964 when Jim Bunning of Philadelphia threw a perfect game against the Mets.

**Q** Who was the 1954 AL rookie of the year?

**A** Pitcher Bob Grim, who went 20-6. He was the first rookie to win 20 games since Russ Ford of New York, 44 years earlier. Grim, who threw primarily fastballs and sliders, had arm problems by his second year and never again approached such excellence.

**Q** The 1954 Yankees won 103 games, the most since 1942. And yet they did not even sniff the postseason. Why?

**A** Because the Cleveland Indians won eight more—although that did not prevent them from getting swept by the New York Giants in the World Series.

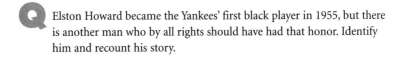

**Q** Elston Howard became the Yankees' first black player in 1955, but there is another man who by all rights should have had that honor. Identify him and recount his story.

**A** Victor Felipe Pellot Pove (better known as Vic Power), a black Puerto Rican, had been in the New York organization since 1951 and did quite well. If a .349 batting average in Triple-A is not evidence of major league talent, what is? Power was also an excellent first baseman. But he was flamboyant, opinionated, and combative when faced with racist behavior. As a result, the Yankees brass decided to ship him off to the Philadelphia A's prior to the 1954 season. In 12 seasons with the A's (who moved to Kansas City the next year), Indians, Twins, and Angels, he played 1,627 games and collected 1,716 hits. Vic Power may have been the most thrown-at batter of his era, and he charged the mound many a time.

**Q** What Negro Leagues team did Elston Howard play for before signing with the Yankees?

**A** The Kansas City Monarchs.

**Q** Who was Joe DiMaggio's wife? Hint: She was a famous Hollywood star. One more hint: She had blond hair.

**A** Marilyn Monroe. The union lasted 274 days—January 14 to October 27, 1954.

**Q** The Cleveland Indians, 1954 AL champs, were riding high late in the '55 season, too. How confident were they?

**A** The Tribe printed and sold tens of thousands of World Series tickets, never thinking the Yankees would catch them, but it happened.

**Q** The 1955 Series had a familiar feel: The Yankees and Dodgers, meeting for the fifth time in nine years. Was there also a familiar ending?

**A** Not this time. Johnny Podres scattered eight hits in a 2-0 shutout in Game 7, giving Brooklyn its first championship since 1900, before the first World Series was held.

**Q** What was the defining play of that Series?

**A** Game 7, seventh inning, Dodgers up by a score of 2-0, two men on. Yogi Berra hit a shot into the left field corner when the Brooklyn outfield had shifted to the right. But left fielder Sandy Amoros—just inserted by manager Walter Alston for defensive purposes—came out of nowhere to catch the ball and, to make matters worse from a New York perspective, threw it to second base to complete a double play. The rally was halted, and the Dodgers proceeded to win.

**Q** Is it true that Rice University once owned Yankee Stadium?

**A** That is a fact. John William Cox, a 1927 Rice graduate, had owned the venue since 1955. Seven years later, he chose to donate the capital stock, plus leasing rights, to his alma mater. And thus this institution of higher education in Houston came to control baseball's Taj Mahal until 1971, at which time New York City exercised its right of eminent domain for a piddling $2.5 million.

**Q** What pitcher had a 13-year career with the Browns, Orioles, Yankees (1955–1962), Los Angeles Angels, and Red Sox?

**A** "Bullet" Bob Turley. In 1958, he went 21-7, won the Cy Young Award, and was MVP in the Yanks' defeat of Milwaukee in the World Series. He later went on to make a fortune in the financial services industry.

**Q** What happened in Yankees history on May 24, 1956?

**A** Mickey Mantle went 5-for-5 in an 11-4 defeat of the Detroit Tigers, raising his batting average to .421.

**Q** The Brooklyn Dodgers had turned the tables on their nemeses from the Bronx in 1955 and had a chance to do it again in the '56 Series. Did they?

**A** No. It went to seven games, but the finale was anticlimactic: Berra had two home runs, Elston Howard had one, and Moose Skowron hit a grand slam in a 9-0 blowout before 33,782 somber fans at Ebbets Field.

**Q** In the 1956 World Series, who batted .350, scored six runs, and hit a homer in Game 3?

**A** Enos "Country" Slaughter. Ten years earlier, he won eternal fame in St. Louis for his "mad dash" to win the 1946 World Series over the Red Sox.

**Q** Who was the last batter at the plate for the Dodgers in Game 5 of the 1956 World Series, when Don Larsen sought to complete a perfect game?

**A** Dale Mitchell, who was called out on strikes by home plate umpire Babe Pinelli. Most observers (including Mitchell) thought the pitch was high and outside.

**Q** It has been said that Larsen was a journeyman who happened to have his best day on baseball's biggest stage. Is it true?

**A** His 81-91 career record says that it is. Casey Stengel used him mostly as a backup starter and occasionally out of the bullpen. And remember that in Game 2 of the '56 Series, he had come on in relief with a 6-0 lead; two innings later, it was 6-4.

**Q** Who was on the mound when the Yankees closed out the Brooklyn Dodgers in the 1956 World Series?

**A** Johnny Kucks. In six seasons (the last two with the Kansas City Athletics), he finished with a 54-56 record.

**Q** Using the fastball, slider, and knuckleball with aplomb, this Yankee won 16 games in both 1956 (including a defeat of the Dodgers in Game 4 of the World Series) and 1957, but he developed a sore arm and began moving from team to team. Who was he?

**A** Tom Sturdivant, who went on to play with eight more clubs before quitting.

**Q** This 5' 6", 139-pound pitcher had been American League MVP in 1952 with Philly (24-7 record) before joining the Yankees for four seasons. By then, he was primarily a reliever. Who was he?

**A** Bobby Shantz. Also an excellent fielder, he won the Gold Glove every year from 1957 to 1964.

**Q** Name the finesse pitcher who won 47 games for the Yanks between 1957 and 1961 but had a hard time breaking into a rotation that included Ford, Shantz, Larsen, and Turley.

**A** Art Ditmar.

**Q** Who was Ryne Duren?

**A** This relief pitcher with poor vision and a blazing fastball came to the Yankees from Kansas City in 1957, as part of the Billy Martin trade. Duren made three All-Star teams in his 11-year career. He had 20 saves in 1958 and a 1.88 ERA the next year. Duren was best known for the extra-thick glasses he wore, an item that only reinforced his reputation for wildness.

**Q** Who was American League rookie of the year in 1957?

**A** Shortstop Tony Kubek, who also hit two home runs in Game 3 of the '57 World Series against the victorious Milwaukee Braves.

**Q** Kubek had a solid nine-year career that ended too early due to back problems. What did he do next?

**A** He spent nearly a quarter-century as an honest and forthright color commentator for NBC, working with such announcers as Jim Simpson, Curt Gowdy, Joe Garagiola, and Bob Costas.

**Q** What was the Copacabana incident?

**A** In May 1957, a group of Yankees met at that posh nightclub to celebrate Billy Martin's 29th birthday. There was a brawl, and GM George Weiss soon sent Martin to the Kansas City A's, believing he was a bad influence on more valuable teammates like Whitey Ford, Yogi Berra, Hank Bauer, and Mickey Mantle—who were also at the Copa that night. Yogi denied it all: "Nobody did nothing to nobody."

**Q** Bill "Moose" Skowron made the final out in the 1957 World Series against the Milwaukee Braves. But he atoned by driving in the winning run in Game 6 of the 1958 Series (also against the Braves) and hit a three-run homer in Game 7 as the Yankees came back from a 3-1 deficit. Where did his athletic career begin?

**A** As a football player at Purdue.

**Q** His defensive miscues made him the goat of Game 4 of the 1958 World Series. Who was he?

**A** Norm Siebern, who lost track of two fly balls in the sixth and seventh innings, letting the Braves score all three of their runs. Siebern would be one of the players traded to Kansas City for Roger Maris prior to the 1960 season.

**Q** He won his fame with the crosstown Giants, was with the Yanks only for parts of 1957 and 1958, and was known as "the Barber" because when he pitched, the batters usually got close shaves. Identify him.

**A** Sal Maglie. Later, as a coach for the Seattle Pilots, he was profiled in a rather unflattering way by Jim Bouton in *Ball Four*.

**Q** This tall, thin Virginian went 39-15 for New York from 1959 until 1962. Who was he?

**A** Jim Coates, who also saved 15 games in relief.

**Q** The 1960 World Series between New York and Pittsburgh was among the strangest ever. How so?

**A** The heavily favored Yankees outscored the Pirates (55-27) and outhit them (91-60) but lost.

**Q** Everybody knows how Game 7 ended, but go ahead and recall it.

**A** The score was tied at 9. In the bottom of the ninth inning, Ralph Terry was pitching and his first batter was the Bucs' second baseman, Bill Mazeroski. He proceeded to drive Terry's second pitch over the left field wall at Forbes Field, sparking a wild celebration in Steeltown. Mickey Mantle later called that loss the most disappointing of his career.

**Q** After losing to Pittsburgh in 1960, Stengel was fired and GM George Weiss was given a nudge. Where did Weiss go for the next half-decade?

**A** He joined Casey across town, becoming president of the expansion New York Mets.

**Q** What native of Panama was an outfielder for New York during the team's pennant-winning years (1960–1964)?

**A** Hector Lopez.

**Q** What was the longest game in Yankees history?

**A** A 22-inning marathon against Detroit in 1961. Jack Reed's two-run homer brought it to a merciful close. In a three-year career, Reed played in 222 games for the Yankees and came to bat 129 times, but that was his only home run.

**Q** This short (5' 8") lefty with a nasty screwball had his best season in 1961: 15-5 with a 2.19 ERA. Who was he?

**A** Luis Arroyo, who also won Game 3 of the World Series against his former team, the Cincinnati Reds.

**Q** What's memorable about John Blanchard?

**A** A defensive liability as a catcher, he made a name for himself as a clutch pinch-hitter. In 1961, he hit 21 homers in 243 at-bats, becoming the first player in history to hit 20 or more in fewer than 250 at-bats. Blanchard was even better in the postseason: His pinch-hit home run in the eighth inning tied Game 3 of the 1961 World Series, setting up another by Roger Maris in a 3-2 New York win over Cincy.

**Q** Name the pitcher who had a combined 28 wins in 1961 and 1962.

**A** Bill Stafford, who won Game 3 of the '62 World Series against the Giants.

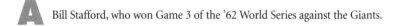

**Q** Who played third base for New York's 1961 World Series team?

**A** Cletis Boyer, one of a trio of brothers (along with Ken and Cloyd) to make it to the majors. Some people considered him the defensive equal of Brooks Robinson of the Orioles, and some of his statistics (putouts, assists, and double plays) back up such an assertion. Independent, outspoken, and a bit of a drinker, Clete Boyer was shipped to Atlanta where he had four more fine years at third base.

**Q** What was baseball's most dramatic story in the summer of 1961?

**A** The friendly duel between teammates Mickey Mantle and Roger Maris, who chased the ghost of Babe Ruth and his 60-homer season of 1927. Had Mantle not been injured in September, he might have come out on top but he still finished with 54. Maris, of course, got his 61st on the last day of the season.

**Q** Who threw the pitch that Maris hit for number 61?

**A** Tracy Stallard of the Red Sox.

**Q** What was the winning players' share in the '61 Series?

**A** $7,389. The losing players' share was $5,356.

**Q** Who was the MVP of that Series?

**A** Pitcher Whitey Ford, who won two games and did not give up a run.

**Q** Ford was never an overpowering pitcher; toward the end of his career (which lasted until 1967), what did he take to doing on the mound?

**A** Scuffing balls to help make them dance; his catcher, Elston Howard, cooperated in that little game, too.

**Q** Who is the Yankees' career leader in victories?

**A** Ford, with 236. Roger Clemens has more wins, of course, but only 77 of them came with New York.

**Q** Roger Maris, American League MVP in 1960 and 1961, later went on to play for what team?

**A** The St. Louis Cardinals, who reached the World Series twice with him in the outfield, winning it once.

**Q** And for whom had Maris played before becoming a Yankee?

**A** The Indians and the A's, from 1957 to 1959.

**Q** Identify the first black pitcher in Yankees history.

**A** That would be Al Downing, a native of Trenton, New Jersey. He was with the team from 1961 to 1969 before moving to Oakland, Milwaukee, and Los Angeles. He won 20 games for the Dodgers in 1971 and, three years later, gave up Hank Aaron's 715th home run.

**Q** Who was the first woman to receive the honor of throwing out the ball on opening day?

**A** Claire Hodgson Ruth, widow of the Bambino himself. She did it in 1962.

**Q** What all-America quarterback at the University of Mississippi was a backup catcher for most of his career (1962–1971) with the Yanks?

**A** Jake Gibbs.

**Q** What is memorable about Tom Tresh?

**A** He played shortstop and in the outfield. In 1962, he was rookie of the year (20 home runs, .286 batting average) and hit a game-winning homer in the World Series against the San Francisco Giants. His father, Mike, had played with the White Sox and Indians from 1938 to 1949. Tresh suffered a knee injury in 1966 and tried to play through it. His numbers started to decline, he became a part-timer, got sent to Detroit, and was out of baseball by 1970.

**89**

**Q** Who was MVP of the 1962 World Series?

**A** Ralph Terry, who pitched a 1-0 shutout in Game 7 over Giants ace Jack Sanford.

**Q** How did the '62 Series end?

**A** There were two outs, with Matty Alou on third and Willie Mays on second. Terry delivered, and Willie McCovey hit a scorching line drive—right at second baseman Bobby Richardson. A couple of feet to either side and they would have been celebrating out in San Fran.

**Q** What was the "City Series?"

**A** Beginning in the 1930s, the Yankees and New York Giants would play an exhibition series against each other in October, when neither was in the World Series. The Yankees and Dodgers had a similar series called the "Mayor's Trophy Game" to benefit sandlot baseball in the New York area. It was revived in 1962 with the birth of the Mets. Due to dwindling interest and bickering between the owners of the two teams, it was halted in the late 1970s.

**Q** This Brooklyn native played first base and was an AL All-Star in 1963, 1964, and 1965, and won the Gold Glove three times. He later played for the Astros, Cubs, Braves, and the Yakult Sparrows in Japan. Who is he?

**A** Joe Pepitone. His life also offers a cautionary tale about talent and money wasted. Legend has it that he got a $25,000 signing bonus in 1962. On his way to spring training, he spent it all on clothes, a Ford Thunderbird, a boat, and a dog. Pepitone arrived in Fort Lauderdale driving the car (with Fido in the back seat), towing the boat, and wearing a sharkskin suit. A free-spirited guy who would go AWOL now and then, he later spent time in prison.

**Q** Identify the 1963 American League MVP.

**A** Elston Howard. He had taken over most of the catching duties from Yogi Berra by then. His numbers were good—a .287 batting average, 28 home runs, 85 RBI, and a Gold Glove. Howard also batted .333 in a losing effort against the Dodgers in the World Series.

**Q** How humiliating was the 1963 World Series for the Yankees?

**A** Extremely. They were ignominiously swept by the Los Angeles Dodgers, courtesy of pitchers Sandy Koufax, Johnny Podres, and Don Drysdale. New York scored four runs, the fewest by any World Series team since the A's in 1905.

**Q** This 6' 6", left-handed reliever once played pro basketball, closed out Game 6 of the 1964 World Series, and had a 1.39 ERA the next year. Who was he?

**A** Steve Hamilton, and let's not forget the "folly floater" pitch he developed late in his career. It was thrown in hesitation delivery, much like the Pirates' Rip Sewell did with his famous "Eephus ball" in the 1940s.

**Q** What else do you remember about the '64 Series?

**A** The Cards' Bob Gibson struck out nine in Game 7, Bobby Richardson had 13 hits, and Mantle cranked his 16th, 17th, and 18th World Series home runs.

**Q** What Yankee was a combat veteran of Bastogne and the Battle of the Bulge, substituted for Yogi Berra at catcher from 1947 to 1954, and then was the manager for three World Series teams—1961, 1962, and 1963?

**A** Ralph Houk, also known as "the Major." After his team lost to the Dodgers in the '63 Series, he moved into the front office, came back to manage for six years, and later led the Tigers and Red Sox. But Houk never again got into the postseason. His career record as a manager was 1,619-1,531.

**Q** One of the strangest turns of events in baseball history came at the end of the 1964 season. What was it?

**A** Johnny Keane managed the St. Louis Cardinals to a National League pennant (thanks to the collapse of the front-running Phillies) and then a World Series title over the Yankees in seven games. Due to problems with owner Augie Busch, Keane announced his resignation almost before the confetti had been cleared from the streets after St. Louis's victory parade. That was only half the story, however. Within a few days, he was presented as the new manager of the Yankees, the very team he had just defeated in the Fall Classic.

**Q** How did Keane do as New York's skipper?

**A** It was a bad match. The Yankees were a team of aging stars, resistant to an outsider. To make matters worse, he replaced Yogi Berra, a Yankee's Yankee if ever there was one. Keane's club finished in sixth place in 1965, and he was fired 20 games into the next season.

**Q** How did Ralph Houk's 1966 Yankees do?

**A** Miserably. They finished in last place in the American League, something that had not happened since 1912.

**Q** What South Carolina native had been one of the best second basemen in the game and was still near his peak when he retired after the '66 season?

**A** Bobby Richardson. His best year came in 1962 when he batted .302, led the league in hits with 209, and finished second to Mantle in MVP voting.

**Q** Who won 39 games (and two more in the World Series) for New York in 1963 and 1964 and later went on to write a candid memoir that detailed major league players' silly shenanigans and use of amphetamines?

**A** Jim Bouton, and the book in question was *Ball Four*. A pariah for three decades, he was finally invited back to an old-timers' game at Yankee Stadium in 1998 and received a thunderous reception.

**Q** How did commissioner Bowie Kuhn characterize *Ball Four*?

**A** He called it "detrimental to baseball."

What was the story with Phil Linz and the harmonica in 1964?

 The Yankees were on the team bus, leaving Comiskey Park after a loss to the White Sox. Linz, a utility infielder, was teaching himself how to play the harmonica. But Berra, in his first year as manager, told him to knock it off. Mickey Mantle, always up for some mischief, urged him to play louder, which he did. That prompted Berra to charge to the back of the bus and slap the offending musical instrument from Linz's hands. The New York press blew a minor incident into a major one, but soon thereafter the Yankees started winning and proceeded to take the pennant. Strangely enough, the light-hitting Linz had two home runs against St. Louis in the World Series.

 Mel Stottlemyre is the father of two sons (Mel Jr. and Todd) who made it to the majors, and he was a coach with the Yanks for four championships. How was he as a player?

 Stottlemyre was called up in the middle of the 1964 season and was soon New York's best pitcher. He faced Bob Gibson three times in the World Series and had three 20-win seasons. Unfortunately, the franchise was entering a decade-long valley and Stottlemyre never played in the postseason again, although he was a tireless workhorse. Diagnosed with multiple myeloma in 1999, he kept on coaching with Joe Torre for six more years. Stottlemyre finally quit in 2005, fed up with the meddlesome George Steinbrenner.

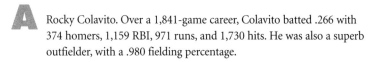 He was born in New York City, and his fondest wish was to join the Yankees. He was playing semipro ball at age nine and soon dropped out of school to pursue his career. A big, strapping man whose good looks did not hurt his image with fans, he served primarily with the Indians and Tigers for 14 years before coming home in the middle of the 1968 season. Who was he?

 Rocky Colavito. Over a 1,841-game career, Colavito batted .266 with 374 homers, 1,159 RBI, 971 runs, and 1,730 hits. He was also a superb outfielder, with a .980 fielding percentage.

He was expected, perhaps unfairly, to follow Mickey Mantle as gracefully as Mantle had done with Joe DiMaggio. But he still had a long and productive career with the Yankees, Giants, Cubs, and then the Yankees again. Name him. Hint: He later served two decades as a team broadcaster.

Bobby Murcer.

Murcer was a good friend of Thurman Munson. After Munson's death in a small airplane crash in 1979, how did Murcer respond?

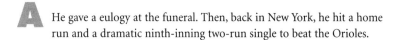 He gave a eulogy at the funeral. Then, back in New York, he hit a home run and a dramatic ninth-inning two-run single to beat the Orioles.

**Q** Roy White played his entire career (1965–1979) with New York. How is he remembered?

**A** White, an outfielder, was a quiet leader in a time when the team was often abysmal. He hit homers from both sides of the plate in the same game five times, he stole 233 bases, and he was steady in the field—not committing a single error in the entire 1975 season. White's patience was rewarded in 1977 and 1978 with back-to-back championships. At 5' 10" and 160 pounds, he was almost certainly the smallest cleanup hitter in the majors for many years.

**Q** This utility infielder, a native of the Virgin Islands, was a bright spot for 10 seasons just when the Yankees were fading. Identify him.

**A** Horace Clarke. His best year was 1969, when he had 183 hits, stole 33 bases, and was the top second baseman in the AL.

**Q** Who spent the last two years (1967 and 1968) of his playing career with the Yankees and later became a successful manager?

**A** Dick Howser. He led New York to the 1980 AL East title before getting canned by Steinbrenner. Howser was with the Kansas City Royals from 1981 to 1986, winning the 1985 World Series.

**Q** This shortstop was nicknamed "Stick," due to his long and lean frame. His 10-year career (1966–1975) began with the Pirates and ended with the Tigers, but he was primarily a Yankee. Identify him.

**A** Gene Michael. As a coach, manager (1981 and 1982), and general manager (1980, 1981, and 1991–1995) in New York, he helped rebuild the farm system and prepare the way for the team's resurgence in the late 1990s. As GM, Michael drafted such players as Bernie Williams, Andy Pettitte, Derek Jeter, and Jorge Posada. He also managed the Cubs for two seasons.

**Q** What Yankees pitcher was 1968 AL rookie of the year?

**A** Stan Bahnsen, who went 17-12, had an ERA of 2.05, and struck out 165 batters.

**Q** He managed the Atlanta Braves from 1978 to 1981, the Toronto Blue Jays from 1982 to 1985, and then went back to Atlanta as an executive and manager again. He has won manager of the year four times and has one World Series ring. Who is he?

**A** Bobby Cox, a stop-gap third baseman for the Yankees in 1968 and 1969. He followed Clete Boyer and preceded Graig Nettles.

**Q** Who made a memorable catch in the 1969 World Series for the Mets and finished out his career with three desultory seasons as a Yankees outfielder?

**A** Ron Swoboda.

**Q** What Yankees pitcher tied an AL record in 1968 by retiring 32 straight batters (over four appearances)?

**A** Lindy McDaniel. In a career that began with the Cardinals in 1955 and ended with the Royals in 1975, he appeared in 987 games and won 119 in relief. McDaniel witnessed some 3,500 major league games and had more than 300 teammates, including Stan Musial, Ernie Banks, Willie Mays, and Mickey Mantle.

**Q** Who was the Yankees' first captain since Lou Gehrig, an All-Star catcher, a hypercompetitive player, and an alumnus of Kent State University?

**A** Thurman Munson, whose career spanned 1969 to 1979. He feuded with Carlton Fisk of the Red Sox and his teammate Reggie Jackson, but he was widely admired and respected. Munson died when his Cessna aircraft crashed in Akron, Ohio. After his funeral, he was honored in an elaborate pre-game ceremony, his number (15) was retired, and plans were made for a bronze bust in Monument Park.

**Q** This tall native of Wenatchee, Washington, had a banner year in 1972, going 16-9 with a 2.40 ERA, but he soon hurt his arm and it was all over. Name him.

**A** Steve Kline.

**Q** What was Ron Blomberg's claim to fame?

**A** A first baseman for the Yankees, Blomberg became the first designated hitter in major league history on April 6, 1973. He faced Red Sox pitcher Luis Tiant in that plate appearance and walked.

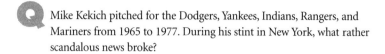

**Q** Mike Kekich pitched for the Dodgers, Yankees, Indians, Rangers, and Mariners from 1965 to 1977. During his stint in New York, what rather scandalous news broke?

**A** That he and fellow Yankees pitcher Fritz Peterson had traded families—both wives, children, and even pets. The two couples had been very close since 1969, and they revealed the odd news in 1973 during spring training. Commissioner Bowie Kuhn said he was appalled but powerless to do anything about it. Both men were hooted handsomely around the American League for the rest of their careers. And, for the record, the trade worked out better for Peterson; he and Susanne (Kekich's ex) married, had four more kids, and are still together, whereas Kekich and Marilyn (Peterson's ex) soon parted ways.

**Q** Peterson was with the team for eight seasons. What kind of numbers did he compile?

**A** He appeared in 265 games for the Yankees, had a record of 109-106, and struck out 893 batters.

**Q** He was with the Yankees for exactly half of his 22-year career, and he made three great plays at third base in Game 3 of the 1978 World Series against the Dodgers. Who was he?

**A** Graig Nettles. The most embarrassing moment in Nettles's life occurred during a game on September 6, 1974. When his bat splintered, it was more than corked—it contained six superballs. Nettles claimed to be as surprised as anyone.

**Q** The number of major league baseball players who attend medical school in the offseason is microscopically small. Name one of them (besides the aforementioned Bobby Brown).

**A** George "Doc" Medich. This big, right-handed pitcher's career spanned 1972 to 1982, and his best work came in 1974 when he won 19 games for the Yankees. Later, while playing for the Texas Rangers, he went into the stands to give CPR to a stricken fan, saving the man's life.

**Q** He was AL rookie of the year for the Kansas City Royals in 1969, even though he had played a few games with Baltimore in 1964 and Cleveland in 1968. He spent 11 seasons as an outfielder with New York, peaking in 1977 with a .330 batting average. Who was he?

**A** Lou Piniella, who managed the Yankees from 1986 to 1988, the Reds from 1990 to 1992 (winning one championship), the Mariners from 1993 to 2002, and the Devil Rays from 2003 to 2005. "Sweet Lou" is now at the helm of the Chicago Cubs.

The straw that stirs the drink—Reggie Jackson in his heyday with the Yankees.

## *Chapter Five*
# THE BOSS TAKES CHARGE

It had been a long stretch of futility for a franchise accustomed to winning. During that 11-year span (1965–1975) without an AL pennant, the Yankees had finished at least 20 games back six times. But things were getting better, as they challenged for the flag in 1972 and 1974. George Steinbrenner's purchase of the team signaled the beginning of a new era. He was willing to invest big money in order to return to the top.

Steinbrenner, who convinced the city to spend $48 million on a two-year refurbishing of Yankee Stadium, signed free agents like Catfish Hunter and Reggie Jackson. Soon, attendance was up and so was media interest in the team. The Yanks were back in the World Series—four times in six years, winning it in 1977 and 1978. Then, although not as suddenly as before, things went bad again. They missed the late Thurman Munson, there were injuries to key players, and many free-agent signings and draft picks did not pan out. The Yankees were at or near the bottom of the AL standings in the early 1990s.

But when general managers Gene Michael and Bob Watson began to shift the team's emphasis from buying free agents to developing young players through its farm system and then keeping them, the results could be seen by 1994. The club had the best record (70-43) in the American League before a players' strike ended the season. The Yankees were back in the playoffs in 1995, at least as a wild card.

**Q** What was George Steinbrenner's sports background?

**A** "The Boss" ran track at Williams College in the early 1950s, was an assistant football coach at Northwestern and Purdue, and owned the Cleveland Pipers of the American Basketball League. A part-owner of the Chicago Bulls, he had sought unsuccessfully to buy the Cleveland Indians.

**Q** What are three of Steinbrenner's more famous quotes?

**A** (1) "Owning the Yankees is like owning the *Mona Lisa*," (2) "I will never have a heart attack—I give them," and (3) "Winning is the most important thing in my life, after breathing. Breathing first, winning next."

**Q** How did the Yanks do in those two years at Shea Stadium?

**A** Quite well. They were 90-69 in their home away from home.

**Q** Billy Martin was hired (and later fired) five times by Steinbrenner. When was the first?

**A** August 1, 1975, when he replaced Bill Virdon.

**Q** Did Bobby Bonds play for the Yankees?

**A** Yes, he did. After spending seven seasons with the San Francisco Giants, Bonds became the Marco Polo of major league baseball. He played for the Yankees in 1975, the Angels in 1976 and 1977, the White Sox and Rangers in 1978, the Indians in 1979, the Cardinals in 1980, and the Cubs in 1981. Bonds, whose combination of power and speed was nearly unmatched, was the father of Barry Bonds of the Pittsburgh Pirates and San Francisco Giants.

**Q** A key figure on the Oakland A's teams that won three titles in the early 1970s, he was one of the first free agents of the modern era, signing with New York for what was then an unprecedented $3.75 million. Identify this big-game pitcher.

**A** Jim "Catfish" Hunter, who finished his 15-year career with 224 wins.

**Q** Who was New York's most consistent starting pitcher from 1976 to 1978?

**A** Ed Figueroa, who won 55 games in those three seasons, the latter two of which ended with a ticker-tape parade in Manhattan. His postseason record was not so good, however: 0-4 in ALCS and World Series games.

**Q** This outfielder had a 17-year career (1969–1985) with seven different teams—the Cubs, Phillies, Indians, Yankees (twice), White Sox (twice), Padres, and Rangers. Who was he? Hint: He wore a famously big afro.

**A** Oscar Gamble. For a man who weighed just 165 pounds, he had a lot of pop, hitting 200 home runs.

**Q** What happened when Chris Chambliss hit one of baseball's most dramatic home runs?

**A** His ninth-inning, Game 5 shot off Kansas City's Mark Littell decided the 1976 AL Championship Series. It snapped a 6-6 tie, ending New York's 12-year pennant drought. The delirious crowd began rushing onto the field almost immediately. Chambliss never made it to third base, much less home. Only later, with a police escort, did he return and touch those two bases to make it official. Against the Royals, Chambliss batted .524 and tied or broke five ALCS records for hits and RBI.

**Q** Identify the Yankees pitcher who went 17-6 in 1976.

**A** Dock Ellis, who also played for the Pirates, Mets, Athletics, and Rangers. He is perhaps best known for the no-hitter he threw against San Diego on June 12, 1970—under the influence of LSD. Ellis later claimed to have never pitched a major league game without the assistance of drugs of one kind or another.

**Q** Billy Martin's 1976 club won the AL by 10 ½ games but got their comeuppance in the World Series. What happened?

**A** The Cincinnati Reds, with such men as Johnny Bench, Pete Rose, Dave Concepcion, George Foster, and Joe Morgan, were far superior, sweeping the series and outscoring the Yanks, 22-8.

**Q** He threw two no-hitters for the Cubs and was a key ingredient of the Oakland Athletics' three titles in the early 1970s. But he was well past his prime during his years with the Yankees (1976–1978). Name this University of Illinois alumnus.

**A** Ken Holtzman, who finished with a 174-150 record over 15 seasons.

**Q** "They're made for each other. One's a born liar, and the other's convicted." Who said these words and to whom did he refer?

**A** They were spoken by Billy Martin in 1976 about his two main antagonists—Reggie Jackson and George Steinbrenner. Martin had recently suspended his right fielder for disobeying a bunt sign, and the other reference was to Steinbrenner who had made an illegal contribution to the 1972 re-election campaign of President Richard Nixon. Needless to say, Martin was fired soon thereafter. A manager who drank too much, an egotistical player, and a meddlesome owner— no wonder the Yankees' clubhouse was called "the Bronx Zoo."

**Q** He was a part-time catcher with the Yankees in 1976 and 1977 whose main contribution was mediating between Martin and Reggie Jackson. Who was he?

**A** Fran Healy, later a broadcaster for both the Yankees and Mets.

**Q** He was a character on a club full of characters, often engaging in verbal duels with teammate Reggie Jackson. In 1976, he hit .312 and stole 43 bases. Who was this native of Miami?

**A** Mickey Rivers. His career spanned 1970 to 1984, roughly divided among the Angels, Yankees, and Rangers.

**Q** He was with the Yankees from 1976 to 1988, was an excellent leadoff man, and could really turn a double play at second. Name him.

**A** Willie Randolph, now serving as manager of the Mets. He played more games at second base (1,688) than anyone else in team history, he was a five-time All-Star, and he walked twice as often as he struck out.

**Q** A superb pitcher for the Indians and Giants from 1961 to 1972, he was a shadow of his former self when the Yankees got him. Who was he?

**A** "Sudden" Sam McDowell, whose fastball, combined with control problems, terrified batters. What might have been a Hall of Fame career was brought down by alcoholism. McDowell later sobered up and said of himself, "I was the biggest, most hopeless, most violent drunk in baseball." In spite of that, he averaged 8.86 strikeouts per nine innings pitched, among the best in the sport's history.

**Q** This speedy center fielder was best known for his work with the Baltimore Orioles, but he contributed to New York's 1977 and 1978 championships. Who was he?

**A** Paul Blair.

**Q** Name the pitcher who was with four consecutive World Series champs—Cincinnati in 1975 and 1976, New York in 1977 and 1978.

**A** Don Gullett. Extensive shoulder and rotator cuff problems ended his career prematurely.

**Q** He had been the Red Sox' bullpen ace before a trade to New York. In his seven years with the Yankees, he made the All-Star team three times, broke the record for career saves, and won the 1977 Cy Young Award. Name him.

**A** Sparky Lyle. Expendable after New York signed Goose Gossage, Lyle finished up with the Rangers, Phillies, and White Sox. Besides being a noted clubhouse prankster, he was a good source of quotes for New York sportswriters. Lyle pitched in 899 games and never started one, so he quipped, "Why pitch nine innings when you can get just as famous pitching two?"

**Q** What was the high point of Reggie Jackson's boisterous five-year stint with the Yanks?

**A** Surely it came on October 18, 1977, in Game 6 of the World Series against the Dodgers. Three swings, three home runs: in the fourth inning off Burt Hooton, in the fifth off Elias Sosa, and in the eighth off Charlie Hough. New York clinched the series that night in Yankee Stadium with an 8-4 victory.

**Q** How did Jackson do in the 1978 postseason?

**A** He batted .462 in the ALCS against the Royals and .391 in the World Series against the Dodgers.

**Q** Ron Guidry (a.k.a. "Louisiana Lightning," a.k.a. "Gator") won more than 20 games three times in his career. What was his best season?

**A** In 1978, the 5' 11", 160-pound lefty was 25-3 with a 1.74 ERA, won the Cy Young Award, and finished second to Boston's Jim Rice in American League MVP voting. Guidry set club records that year in strikeouts (248) and won his first 13 starts. That included a 4-0 win at Yankee Stadium in which he had 18 strikeouts against the California Angels.

**Q** What was the Boston Massacre?

**A** The Yankees' four-game sweep of the Red Sox in early September 1978 (by the scores of 15-3, 13-2, 7-0, and 7-4), a crushing series of defeats for Don Zimmer's team in a heated pennant race.

**Q** Bucky Dent's homer against the Red Sox in a playoff game is among the more memorable events in franchise history. What were the circumstances when the New York shortstop bopped the ball over Fenway Park's Green Monster?

**A** The Yankees had been 14 games behind the Red Sox in July, but they began to win and Boston began to lose. Then the Sox won their last eight games, tying the Yanks and setting up a one-game playoff. It was the seventh inning, a fierce wind was blowing out to left field, and Mike Torrez threw the fateful pitch. BoSox fans still rue the day—October 2, 1978.

**Q** Did Steinbrenner ever hire Dent to manage?

**A** In fact, he did. Dent was the Yanks' skipper in late 1989 and early 1990, with a record of 36-53. It didn't work out.

**Q** Outfielder Jay Johnstone, who had a 20-year major league career, spent parts of 1978 and 1979 with the Yankees. What was he known for?

**A** Johnstone kept teammates entertained with his goofy clubhouse antics. He was a broadcaster with the team in the late 1980s.

**Q** It was Game 2 of the 1978 World Series against the Dodgers. The bases were loaded with two outs in the bottom of the ninth, with Reggie Jackson at the plate. Amid this high drama, a rookie pitcher struck out Mr. October. Who was he?

**A** Bob Welch. But Jackson got his revenge on Welch in the deciding sixth game, hitting a home run.

**Q** This relief pitcher's fastball and curve were both hellacious. His career began in 1972 with the White Sox and ended in 1994 with the Mariners. He was at his best with the Yankees from 1978 to 1983, however. Name him.

**A** Rich "Goose" Gossage, who won 124 games and saved 310.

**Q** This Kentuckian was a reserve second baseman with just 10 hits and no RBI in the 1978 season, but he got hot at the right time, going 7-for-16 in the World Series. Who was he?

**A** Brian Doyle.

**Q** What big right-hander had a rookie-record 14 relief wins in 1979?

**A** Ron Davis, who was dealt to the Twins in 1982. There, he had four straight seasons with at least 22 saves. Davis was a one-dimensional pitcher; he had little to offer besides a hard fastball. When it failed him, he got rocked.

**Q** This man had a 25-year career (1959–1983), primarily with the Washington Senators/Minnesota Twins. By the time he got to the Bronx, he was pitching on guile alone. Who was he?

**A** Jim Kaat, who appeared in 44 games for the Yanks in 1979 and 1980.

**Q** Name the pitcher on whom revolutionary surgery was performed, allowing him to keep going and going and going.

**A** Tommy John. He was with six different teams in a 26-year career—including the Yanks from 1979 to 1982 and 1986 to 1989. In 1974, while with the Dodgers, he permanently damaged the ulnar collateral ligament in his pitching arm (he was a lefty). Dr. Frank Jobe replaced that ligament with a tendon from John's right arm. After an entire year in rehab, John came back and found that he could pitch remarkably well. It opened up a brave new world in which some pitchers now actually *choose* to have "Tommy John surgery."

**Q** The Yankees had to find a top-flight catcher after Thurman Munson's death in 1979. What did they do?

**A** They got Rick Cerone in a trade with Toronto. His best year was 1980 when he was behind the plate for 147 games, batted .277, and had 14 homers. Cerone actually had three stints with New York and retired in 1992. But he stayed in the organization and is now the director of public relations.

**Q** Name the Cuban-born right-hander who won 21 games for New York in 1979 and 1980.

**A** Luis Tiant, who is perhaps best known for his work as a member of the Boston Red Sox.

**Q** He hit a three-run bomb in Game 1 of the 1981 World Series against the Dodgers. Name him.

**A** Bob Watson, who had spent most of his playing career with Houston. He later served as GM of both the Astros and Yankees.

**Q** He was AL rookie of the year in 1981, but by '84 he had been moved (against his will) to the bullpen—and was even better than as a starter. Who was he?

**A** Dave Righetti.

**Q** Gene Michael and Bob Lemon split managerial duties in the strike-shortened 1981 season, which found New York and Los Angeles in the World Series. Did the Yankees prevail?

**A** It appeared they would after taking the first two games, but the Dodgers won the next four. The most lamentable performance in that Series would be a tossup between pitcher George Frazier, who lost three games, and Dave Winfield, who had one hit in 22 at-bats.

**Q** What did Steinbrenner call Winfield afterward?

**A** "Mr. May," in contrast to his long-time favorite, Reggie Jackson, whom he had dubbed "Mr. October."

**Q** Winfield was an alumnus of the University of Minnesota, was drafted in three different sports (baseball, basketball, and football), collected more than 3,000 hits and got into Cooperstown in 2001, his first year of eligibility. What other teams did he play for?

**A** The Padres, Angels, Blue Jays, Twins, and Indians.

**Q** He joined the Yankees in 1982 in the middle of a solid 19-year career, but he was soon overshadowed by the exploits of his son. Identify him.

**A** Ken Griffey Sr. Father and son were briefly teammates with Seattle in 1991.

**Q** What second baseman was NL rookie of the year with the Dodgers in 1982 and spent three years in New York?

**A** Steve Sax, who was five times an All-Star until he developed a case of the "yips" in which his throwing mechanics broke down; Sax had 30 errors—most of them throwing errors—in one season.

**Q** He was another National League rookie of the year, in this case with the Giants in 1975. This pitcher made predictions and usually backed them up. His act had worn a bit thin by the time he played with the Yankees (1983–1986), but he could still pitch. Who was he?

**A** John "the Count" Montefusco.

**Q** This player did not show much in his rookie year of 1983, because the Yankees soon got rid of him. But in a 17-season career, he had a .270 average, stole 620 bases, and was a fine outfielder. Who was he?

**A** Otis Nixon, who also played with the Indians, Expos, Braves, Red Sox, Rangers, Blue Jays, and Twins.

**Q** Bert Campaneris was one of the most intriguing players in the second half of the twentieth century. Was he ever with the Yankees?

**A** Campy, who was born in Cuba, did have a final hurrah with Billy Martin's club in 1983, batting .322 in 60 games. A key figure in the Oakland Athletics' three championships in the early 1970s, he could hit, steal bases, play defense, and do virtually anything else to help his team win. In one game in 1965, he rotated positions each inning—including that of pitcher.

**Q** It was a lovely Sunday afternoon in the summer of 1983. New York and Kansas City were playing at Yankee Stadium, and the Royals, behind by one run, were down to their last out. Then George Brett hit a two-run homer off Goose Gossage. What happened next?

**A** Yankees manager Billy Martin went to home plate umpire Tim McClelland and cited an obscure rule, which stated that pine tar on a bat could go no higher than 18 inches. Brett's bat had 24 inches of the sticky stuff. McClelland dutifully nullified the home run—meaning the game was over and the Yanks had won—prompting Brett to charge the ump like a mad bull. Seemingly, half the Royals were needed to restrain him. KC protested, and American League president (and former Yankees chief executive) Lee McPhail concurred. The game was replayed three weeks later, starting after Brett's homer, and the Royals won, 5-4. The "pine-tar game," and Brett's volcanic response to the initial call, have become part of baseball lore.

**Q** Don Baylor had a long career—19 seasons—and was with the Yanks from 1983 to 1985. How did he do then?

**A** Baylor's .303 batting average in 1983 was his best ever. A power hitter who often crowded the plate, he was fearless about getting hit by pitches. By the time he retired, Baylor had 338 homers, 2,135 hits, and 285 stolen bases. He won a World Series title with the Twins in 1987, and later managed the Colorado Rockies and Chicago Cubs.

**Q** This slow-footed, switch-hitting catcher played seven seasons with the Twins before coming to New York. Who was he? Hint: He was behind the plate for Dave Righetti's no-hitter in 1983.

**A** Butch Wynegar.

**Q** What third baseman played for the Yankees from 1984 to 1989 but never won a championship until he was with the Minnesota Twins in 1991?

**A** Mike Pagliarulo.

**Q** When Don Mattingly won the AL batting title in 1984 (with a .343 average), no Yankee had won it since when?

**A** 1956, when Mickey Mantle hit .353.

 He only played five years in New York (1985–1989), but he is the franchise leader in stolen bases, with 326. Who was he?

 Rickey Henderson.

Q What else did Henderson do in his long (1979–2003), quirky career?

A He had a very high on-base percentage, hit home runs like few other leadoff batters, and was durable. Some of his teammates and managers loved him, and some definitely did not. Lou Piniella and Dallas Green were two of the latter. Henderson often referred to himself in the third person, made extra-fancy "snatch catches," and took his sweet time strolling around the bases after home runs.

Q For how many major league teams did Henderson play in his career?

A Nine: The A's (four times), Yankees, Blue Jays, Padres (twice), Angels, Mets, Mariners, White Sox, and Dodgers. He scored 2,295 runs and stole 1,406 bases—both all-time records.

Q Name the 6' 7" lefty who went 18-6 in 1986 for New York.

A Dennis Rasmussen.

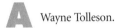 What fleet, slap-hitting infielder who played with the Yankees in the late 1980s had been an all-America wide receiver at Western Carolina University?

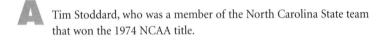 Wayne Tolleson.

 This big right-handed pitcher, who was with the Yankees in 1987 and 1988, had a basketball background. Who was he and what was his hoops connection?

Tim Stoddard, who was a member of the North Carolina State team that won the 1974 NCAA title.

In the summer of 1987, this man tied a major league record by hitting home runs in eight straight games—with a total of 10 dingers in that streak. He set a record of his own that year by hitting six grand slams. He was a terror from 1984 to 1988, batting between .311 and .352, seldom striking out, and playing a stellar first base. But horseplay with a teammate in the locker room caused a back injury that never fully healed, leading to his premature retirement in 1995. Most baseball historians say he is the best Yankee never to have played in a World Series game. So who is he?

Don Mattingly.

**Q** This right-handed pitcher's rookie year was fairly pedestrian, so the Yanks traded him to Pittsburgh in 1987. He blossomed with the Pirates, capped by a Cy Young Award in 1990 when he went 22-6 with a 2.76 ERA. Who was he?

**A** Doug Drabek.

**Q** This Panamanian was supposed to be the next great pinstripe-clad centerfielder when he arrived in 1987, but it never quite happened—due to injuries, complacency, or other issues often speculated about in the New York tabloids. Who was he?

**A** Roberto Kelly. His best year may have been 1989, when he batted .302 and drove in 48 runs. He was, it should be added, a fine man with the glove at all three outfield spots.

**Q** This outfielder was with New York for a total of 32 games in 1987 and 1988, but his numbers were mediocre, so he was shipped to Seattle. In 13 years as a Mariner, he hit 307 home runs. Who was he?

**A** Jay Buhner. Not only could he bat, but he had a rocket for an arm. It was one of the Yankees' worst trades of that period.

**Q** This 6' 6", 205-pounder was one of the top pitchers of his era, at least when he could avoid injury. His last year as a full-time starter was 1988, when he went 13-7 for the Yankees. Name him.

**A** John Candelaria, best remembered for his work with Pittsburgh.

**Q** His major league pitching career started in 1987 with the Yankees and finished in 2005, again with the Yankees. Most of the years in between were with other teams, including World Series winners at Toronto (1992 and 1993) and Florida (1997). He also threw a no-hitter for the Marlins in 1995. Who was he?

**A** Al Leiter.

**Q** Billy Martin was fired for the fifth and final time on June 23, 1988. Who replaced him?

**A** Lou Piniella, who was on his second go-round as the Yanks' skipper. Martin, by the way, would die in a car accident 18 months later.

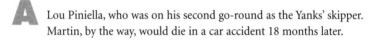

**Q** What other teams did Martin manage?

**A** The Minnesota Twins, Detroit Tigers, Texas Rangers, and Oakland Athletics.

**Q** He is known primarily for his exploits on the football field (defensive back at Florida State, then with the Atlanta Falcons, San Francisco 49ers, Dallas Cowboys, Washington Redskins, and Baltimore Ravens), but he also played baseball for the Yankees, Braves, Reds, and Giants in his spare time. Who might he be?

**A** "Neon" Deion Sanders. He participated in just 71 games with the Yanks—14 in 1989 and 57 in 1990. He is the only man to have played in a major league baseball game and an NFL game on the same day, and the only one to play in a World Series and a Super Bowl.

**Q** Manager Dallas Green was blunt and an admitted screamer. He had won a World Series with the Phillies in 1980, although most of his players detested him. What happened in Green's one year (1989) with the Yankees?

**A** It was actually a bit less than one year. With his club playing .463 ball, Green insulted Steinbrenner by referring to him as "Manager George." He was soon shown the door.

**Q** What outfielder was NL rookie of the year with Atlanta in 1990, married film actress Halle Berry three years later, and won a championship with the Braves and another with the Yankees?

**A** David Justice, most valuable player of the 2000 ALCS against Seattle. He also played with the Indians, Mets, and A's in his 14-year career.

**Q** In 1981, he pitched in three games to help the Dodgers beat New York in the World Series. Who was he?

**A** Steve Howe, a Yankee from 1991 to 1996. A hard-throwing lefty, he was also plagued by drug and alcohol abuse; over the course of a 17-year career, Howe would be suspended seven times. He died on April 28, 2006, in a one-car accident, and the coroner's report showed methamphetamine in his bloodstream.

**Q** He was a feared home-run hitter with the Kansas City Royals, so New York signed him to a big free-agent contract in 1992. He hit 75 home runs over the next three seasons, but lousy defense, high strikeout numbers, and injuries limited his success. Who was he?

**A** Danny Tartabull, whose father, Jose, was a major leaguer from 1962 to 1970.

**Q** He had been New York's starting shortstop for three years, but when Derek Jeter arrived it was adios. Identify him.

**A** Randy Velarde, who later played with the Angels and A's.

**Q** Who was Jim Abbott?

**A** To start with the most obvious, he was a left-handed pitcher who was born without a right hand. That did not deter him, however. Abbott excelled in high school not only as a pitcher but as a quarterback. He had three very good years at the University of Michigan and got to the majors in 1989 with the California Angels. The high point of his career came on September 4, 1993, when he was with the Yankees— he threw a no-hitter against the Cleveland Indians. Despite his physical limitations, Abbott was an above-average fielder. He also spent one season with the Milwaukee Brewers of the National League, where he got two hits in 21 at-bats.

**Q** With the Red Sox, he led the American League in hitting five times and had more than 200 hits every season from 1984 to 1989. But he never got a ring until 1996 with the Yankees. To whom do we refer?

**A** Wade Boggs, who spent five years in New York. After the final out of Game 6 of the '96 World Series, he joined a mounted police officer and took an unforgettable ride around the perimeter of the field at Yankee Stadium.

**Q** What very talented 6' 6" outfielder helped the Mets win the 1986 title and also played for the Dodgers, Giants, and Yankees?

**A** Darryl Strawberry, who was the 1983 NL rookie of the year, an eight-time All-Star, and author of 335 home runs. But he was a poster boy for immature, overpaid pro athletes. Strawberry's list of legal and personal problems is quite long—such as missing games, domestic abuse, alcohol abuse, drug abuse, tax evasion, soliciting sex from a policewoman posing as a prostitute, and car crashes. He was with the Yankees for five seasons, playing 32 games in 1995, 63 in 1996, 11 in 1997, 101 in 1998, and 24 in 1999. Unfulfilled potential, thy name is Darryl Strawberry.

**Q** What happened in Yankees' history on August 10, 1995?

**A** Catcher Mike Stanley hit three homers and had seven RBI, but it was not enough to keep his team from losing to the Indians, 10-9.

Shortstop Derek Jeter, one of the best all-around players of the past decade.

## *Chapter Six*
# YANKEES CLIMB THE MOUNTAIN AGAIN

People who knew baseball could see that changes were afoot in the Bronx by the mid-1990s. Joe Torre was hired as manager, although the media initially did not seem impressed with George Steinbrenner's pick. They soon had reason to change their opinions; Torre's team won it all in 1996, and then again in 1998, 1999, and 2000. And several near-misses followed.

The '98 Yankees were the best of the bunch—although Roger Clemens had not yet arrived. Fuzzy-cheeked GM Brian Cashman built upon the foundation already laid by his predecessors, and a host of talented players have now won nine straight AL East championships. First among that group would have to be Derek Jeter, then how about Bernie Williams, Andy Pettitte, Jorge Posada, and Mariano Rivera? They, and their teammates, need not blush about being mentioned in the same breath with, for example, Casey Stengel's 1961 club (Whitey Ford, Mickey Mantle, Roger Maris, Elston Howard, and Bobby Richardson), Joe McCarthy's 1939 club (Joe DiMaggio, Red Ruffing, Lefty Gomez, Bill Dickey, and Frankie Crosetti), and even Miller Huggins's 1927 club (Babe Ruth, Lou Gehrig, Tony Lazzeri, Waite Hoyt, and Urban Shocker).

No doubt, the dynasty has been rejuvenated. Crowds are bigger when the Yankees visit Baltimore, Arlington, Seattle, Oakland, or other American League outposts. And at home, attendance has never been better—more than 4.2 million fans packed Yankee Stadium in 2006. The New York franchise is the wealthiest in major league baseball, which is reflected in a payroll that now stands at $210 million per year.

**Q** How did shortstop Derek Jeter do in 1995 when he was called up from the minors?

**A** He was sent back down after 13 games but was back in New York to stay in 1996.

**Q** Jeter and what other Yankee scored more than 100 runs in their first four full seasons?

**A** Joe DiMaggio. The Yankee Clipper fell a bit short of that mark in his fifth year, but Jeter did not.

**Q** Did Jeter have a good year in 2000?

**A** He did. Jeter was named MVP of the All-Star Game and of the World Series that year. Needless to say, he was on the winning team in both instances.

**Q** What kind of money did Jeter make in 2005?

**A** His salary was $18.9 million, and he earned another $5 million in endorsements.

**Q** What more can be said about Jeter?

**A** He was named captain of the team in 2003 for good reason. As a batter, shortstop, and baserunner, Jeter is a superlative player. He also has the respect of his coaches, teammates, and opponents. On top of all that, he is photogenic.

**Q** His career is not yet over, and some people already consider him the best closer the game has seen. Who is he?

**A** Mariano Rivera, a native of Panama. Really a master of the cut fastball, he was World Series MVP in 1999 and has saved more than 400 games. Even the best fail now and then, as he did in the ninth inning of Game 7 of the 2001 World Series. Luis Gonzalez hit a bloop single to win the game and the Series for the Diamondbacks. Nevertheless, Rivera's legacy grew with great seasons in 2003, 2004, and 2005.

**Q** What kind of player was Joe Torre?

**A** He caught and played third base and first base. In 18 years with the Braves, Cardinals, and Mets, the Brooklyn native had a .297 batting average and hit 252 home runs. His peak came in 1971 when he was National League MVP for St. Louis. His worst day as a player may have come on July 25, 1975, when he ground into four double plays against the Astros.

**Q** And how about Torre, the manager?

**A** He was with the Mets from 1977 to 1981, the Braves from 1982 to 1984, and the Cards from 1990 to 1995. With those three teams (the same ones for which he had played), he had a fairly pedestrian record, although Atlanta won the NL Western Division title in 1982. If he had critics, he silenced them with a World Series crown that first year and three more from 1998 to 2000. Some people still debate how hard it is to manage a team with such a huge payroll, but one fact remains— Torre is the longest-tenured Yankees manager during George Steinbrenner's ownership of the franchise.

**Q** Name the most valuable player of the 1996 ALCS against Baltimore.

**A** Bernie Williams.

**Q** What incident from that series gained instant notoriety?

**A** In Game 1, the Yankees were trailing the Orioles, 4-3, in the bottom of the eighth when Derek Jeter hit a ball to deep right field. Tony Tarasco of the O's may have caught it, but he never got the chance; 12-year-old Jeffrey Maier reached over and deflected the ball into the stands. Right field umpire Rich Garcia mistakenly called it a home run instead of spectator interference, despite Baltimore's vehement protestations. New York went on to win the game in the 11th inning.

**Q** The defending champion Atlanta Braves had won the last three games of the NLCS by a 32-1 margin and were heavily favored to take the trophy again in 1996, New York's first World Series in 15 years. Did they?

**A** They did not. Jim Leyritz's home run in Game 4 shifted the momentum, and Series MVP John Wetteland saved four games.

**Q** This burly first baseman hit most of his 319 homers for the Detroit Tigers, but he was with the Yanks when they won the 1996 World Series. Who was he?

**A** Cecil Fielder, whose life later unraveled due to gambling problems. His son, Prince, now plays for the Milwaukee Brewers.

**Q** His nickname was "Rock," and he played for the Yankees from 1996 to 1998. He was also with the Expos, White Sox, Orioles, and Marlins in a 23-year career. Who was he?

**A** Tim Raines, whose career numbers look like this: .294 batting average, 170 home runs, 980 RBI, 1,571 runs scored, 808 stolen bases, 430 doubles, and 113 triples. He could wreak havoc on the basepaths, even more so than Rickey Henderson.

**Q** NL rookie of the year in 1984 and Cy Young Award winner in 1985, this guy had a 98-mph fastball and a sweeping curve. He was on a fast track to being among the greatest ever before drugs, alcohol, and assorted legal issues took hold. Who was he?

**A** Dwight "Doc" Gooden. A member of the Mets from 1984 to 1994, he was out of baseball in 1995 before joining the Yankees for two seasons. He managed to throw a no-hitter against Seattle on May 14, 1996, even as his decline continued. Gooden was also with the Indians, Astros, and Devil Rays before his career ended in 2001. Consider that of his 194 victories, more than half came before age 25.

**Q** This Texas A&M grad was rookie of the year with the Twins in 1992 and played for the Yanks from 1997 to 2001. He was an excellent hitter, base-stealer, and second baseman before developing an odd inability to throw accurately. Name him.

**A** Chuck Knoblauch. He inexplicably could not throw well in the field, sometimes sailing the ball 20 or 30 feet over his teammates' heads. Advice from coaches, sports psychologists, friends, and the media were to no avail. Knoblauch never fully recovered his throwing arm and was eventually moved to the outfield. He spent one season in Kansas City before retiring.

**Q** Known as a bit of a free-swinger when he was with Cincinnati, Paul O'Neill came to the Yankees in 1993 and changed that reputation completely. What was his finest hour?

**A** It had to be the 1997 ALCS, which New York lost to Cleveland. His batting average for that series was .421.

**Q** This first baseman spent five years with the Seattle Mariners before coming to New York. Although he was replacing the popular Don Mattingly, he won over the fans and was a key player on the 1996, 1998, 1999, and 2000 championship teams. Name him.

**A** Tino Martinez. In seven seasons with the Yankees, he hit 192 homers and drove in 739 runs.

**Q** This left-handed pitcher, a native of Baton Rouge, Louisiana, played nine seasons with the Yankees before signing a big contract with the Houston Astros. Who is he?

**A** Andy Pettitte, MVP of the 2003 AL Championship Series.

**Q** What Yankees pitcher attained instant immortality by throwing a perfect game on May 17, 1998?

**A** David "Boomer" Wells. This outstanding but well-traveled (Blue Jays [twice], Tigers, Reds, Orioles, White Sox, Padres, and Red Sox, along with the Yankees [also twice]) player with a lifelong interest in Babe Ruth had his best year in 1998. He rang up an 18-4 record, came in third in Cy Young Award voting, had that perfecto against the Minnesota Twins, and was named most valuable player of the ALCS over Cleveland, winning two games. Wells and a ghostwriter combined on a 2003 autobiography in which he claimed to have been hung over when he threw his perfect game, made various disparaging comments, and speculated about which of his fellow major leaguers might be using steroids.

 Identify the Japanese pitcher who won two rings (1998 and 1999) with the Yankees and once so infuriated Steinbrenner that the Boss called him a "fat pussy toad."

**A** Hideki Irabu.

**Q** How many games did the Yankees win in 1998?

**A** An American League record of 114. The previous mark of 111 by the 1948 Cleveland Indians was when the schedule was just 154 games, not 162. Including the postseason, New York won 125 games in 1998.

**Q** How did it go for the San Diego Padres in the 1998 World Series?

**A** Not so well. The Yankees put the wood to them in a four-game blowout.

**Q** Joe Torre's '98 team was one of the best in the modern era, so name his typical starting nine.

**A** Jorge Posada at catcher, Tino Martinez at first base, Chuck Knoblauch at second base, Derek Jeter at shortstop, Scott Brosius at third base, Chad Curtis in left field, Bernie Williams in center field, and Paul O'Neill in right field. The starting pitchers were David Cone, Orlando Hernandez, Hideki Irabu, Andy Pettitte, and David Wells. They played before 2,955,193 fans at home, and their salaries ranged from $170,000 to $8.3 million.

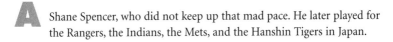

**Q** He was a native of Key West, Florida, and was 26 years old when he got a call to join the Yankees. He was extremely productive in the final 27 games of the 1998 season—batting .373, hitting 10 home runs (including three grand slams), and getting 27 ribbies. Who was this person?

**A** Shane Spencer, who did not keep up that mad pace. He later played for the Rangers, the Indians, the Mets, and the Hanshin Tigers in Japan.

**Q** This slick-fielding third baseman was acquired from the Oakland A's in 1998 and turned in some stellar performances over the next four years. Who was he?

**A** Scott Brosius. In 1998, despite batting eighth or ninth in the order, he had a .300 average with 98 RBI and 19 home runs. He was World Series MVP that year. Brosius had a dream come true in Game 5 of the 2001 Series against the Arizona Diamondbacks, hitting a two-out, two-run homer in the bottom of the ninth and setting up a Yankees win.

**Q** Drafted by New York in the 24th round of the 1990 amateur draft, this man is a switch-hitting catcher. Who is he?

**A** Jorge Posada, a member of the World Series winners of 1998, 1999, and 2000. In 2003, he hit 30 home runs, batted .281, and drove in 101 runs.

**Q** This big-boned Texan had won 233 games for Boston and Toronto, but he had no World Series rings to show for it. Then he joined Torre's Yanks in 1999 and that changed. You know who he is, but name him anyway.

**A** Seven-time Cy Young Award winner Roger Clemens. He stayed in New York for five years before moving on to the Houston Astros in 2004.

**Q** Where did Clemens attend college?

**A** The University of Texas. He was 25-7 in two seasons with the Longhorns, winners of the 1983 College World Series. But it is safe to say that nobody had the slightest idea Clemens would turn out to be such a great pitcher in the pros. After all, 18 players were chosen ahead of him in the amateur draft.

**Q** He was with the Yankees in 1999 and 2000 (Phillies, Indians, and Angels before, Royals, Orioles, and Diamondbacks later), and he was a fair pitcher. Who is he, and why is he remembered at all?

**A** He is Jason Grimsley, and he confessed to using human growth hormone, amphetamines, and steroids throughout his baseball career.

**Q** He was a member of Cuba's gold-medal-winning team in the 1992 Barcelona Olympics, defected from the island in 1997, and was most valuable player of the 1999 ALCS against Boston. Who is this pitcher with the corkscrew windup?

**A** Orlando "El Duque" Hernandez. He later pitched for the Expos, White Sox, and Diamondbacks.

**Q** What happened at Yankee Stadium on Yogi Berra Day, July 18, 1999?

**A** David Cone threw the 16th perfect game in baseball history. The victims were the Montreal Expos. Cone was then in his 14th season in the majors and had lost some speed on his fastball, but he compensated with savvy.

**Q** For what other teams did Cone play?

**A** The Kansas City Royals (he was a KC native), New York Mets, Toronto Blue Jays, and Boston Red Sox. The winner of the 1994 Cy Young Award, he had a 194-126 record with 2,668 strikeouts. He was a big-game pitcher who had a reputation for leading his teams to the postseason. This is one reason Cone was traded so much—he was always a hot commodity for contending teams.

 This native of the Dominican Republic actually started his pro baseball career in Japan before joining the Yanks in 1999. He played with New York for five seasons, the best of which came in 2002: 696 at-bats, 209 hits, 92 extra-base hits, 41 stolen bases, and 128 runs scored. He also set a team record for strikeouts (157). Name this productive second baseman.

Alfonso Soriano.

Soriano later served as trade bait for whom?

Alex Rodriguez. The Yankees sent Soriano and a minor leaguer to the Texas Rangers for A-Rod and $67 million of the $179 million left on the latter's contract.

What was the final game of the 20th century?

On October 27, 1999, the Yanks completed a four-game sweep of the Atlanta Braves to capture their 25th World Series title. It was also New York's 12th straight win in World Series play, tying a record set by the 1927, 1928, and 1932 Yankees.

What else of note happened in that '99 Series?

Before Game 2, NBC reporter Jim Gray did a contentious interview with Pete Rose, urging him to admit that he had bet on baseball games. That set off a debate among fans and the media as to whether Gray was right or wrong, and why Rose wouldn't go ahead and fess up (which he later did). After Chad Curtis hit a walkoff homer in Game 3, he snubbed Gray on camera, drawing the wrath of both Steinbrenner and Torre. Curtis was soon shipped out of the Bronx.

**Q** How much did the Yankees get for winning the 1999 championship?

**A** A cool $326,000 each.

**Q** Joe DiMaggio died in 1999. In the last few years of his life, what was the stipulation for all his public appearances?

**A** He had to be introduced as "the greatest living ballplayer."

**Q** He was one of the "Bruise Brothers" with the Oakland A's, one of nine major league teams on his résumé. He hit 462 homers, had an endless series of run-ins with the law, and blew the whistle on the use of steroids—his own and that of fellow players. Who was he?

**A** None other than Jose Canseco, a member of the 2000 World Series champion New York Yankees.

**Q** The 2000 Yankees won just 87 games in the regular season (down from 114 in 1998 and 98 in 1999), but they took the pennant, then edged Oakland and Seattle en route to the World Series. What happened there?

**A** In the first Subway Series since 1956, the Yankees beat the New York Mets, four games to one.

**Q** What memorable event took place in Game 2 of that Series?

**A** Roger Clemens was on the mound, and the Mets' Mike Piazza was at the plate. Piazza hit a broken-bat foul ball in which the barrel of the bat came to Clemens. He flung it contemptuously in Piazza's direction. There had been bad blood between the two: Piazza was 7 for 12 against Clemens entering that game, and Clemens had beaned Piazza in an interleague game in the summer. The incident touched off a near-brawl, and while the umpires did not eject the Yankees pitcher, he was later fined $50,000.

**Q** A role player was a hero in Game 5 of the 2000 World Series against the Mets. Who is he, and what did he do?

**A** He is Luis Sojo, a native of Barquisimeto, Venezuela. In that game, the score was tied, 2-2, in the ninth inning, and there were two outs when Sojo delivered a two-RBI single off Al Leiter, winning the Series.

**Q** This heavily tattooed first baseman debuted with the Oakland A's in 1995, was league MVP in 2000, and soon joined the Yanks in a seven-year, $120 million deal. Name him.

**A** Jason Giambi. Later came allegations that he used steroids and human growth hormone, and there was a rambling press conference in which he apologized but failed to say for what. Nevertheless, Giambi enjoyed a surprising renaissance in 2005 and 2006.

**Q** This right-handed pitcher had been a Baltimore Oriole for a decade before joining the Yanks. On September 2, 2001, in a game against the Red Sox, he flirted with perfection, retiring his first 26 batters before giving up a bloop single. Name him.

**A** Mike Mussina, who would win 77 games for New York from 2001 to 2005. Mussina, by the way, has a football background. He was a place-kicker at Stanford in the late 1980s.

**Q** The three-time champs were back in the World Series in 2001, this time against the Arizona Diamondbacks, a team in its fourth year of existence. Who won?

**A** That was a thrilling Series, with two extra-inning games and three late-inning comebacks, and it went the full seven before Arizona prevailed. Games 3, 4, and 5 were in New York, a city still in shock from the September 11 terrorist attacks seven weeks earlier. President George Bush wore a bulletproof vest when throwing out the ceremonial first pitch. Game 7 featured Clemens versus Curt Schilling of the Diamondbacks. It ended in the ninth inning when Luis Gonzales's single drove in Jay Bell with the winning run.

**Q** He was a Yankee from 1992 to 1995, spent time in Seattle, San Diego (he was most valuable player of the NLCS for the Padres in '98), and St. Louis, and was back in New York in 2001 when he won Game 5 of the World Series. Name him.

**A** Sterling Hitchcock.

**Q** Who was the Yankees' manager on September 28, 2003, when Wells earned the 200th win of his career?

**A** New York had already won its division and, on the last day of the regular season, Joe Torre handed the reins to Roger Clemens. Wells pitched 7 $\frac{2}{3}$ innings before being removed by manager Clemens, whose bench coach was erstwhile pitcher Andy Pettitte.

**Q** What was Aaron Boone's biggest moment in pinstripes?

**A** It came in Game 7 of the ALCS against the Boston Red Sox in 2003. In the 11th inning, Tim Wakefield threw a knuckleball that Boone deposited over the left field wall at Yankee Stadium. He circled the bases and got an uproarious welcome at home plate from his teammates, who knew they were going to the World Series—and the Sox weren't.

**Q** Boone came from quite a baseball family. Can you name the other major league Boones?

**A** Aaron's grandfather is Ray Boone (1948–1960, with the Indians, Tigers, White Sox, A's, Braves, and Red Sox), his father is Bob Boone (1972–1990, with the Phillies, Angels, and Royals), and his brother is Bret Boone (1992–2005, with the Mariners, Reds, Braves, Padres, Mariners again, and Twins). It is the first three-generation family in major league baseball history.

**Q** And how did it go in that '03 World Series?

**A** New York's opponents were the Florida Marlins. The NL upstarts had a $54 million payroll, roughly one-third that of the Yankees, but they won it, 4-2. The Series MVP was Florida pitcher Josh Beckett.

**Q** He played seven seasons with the Seattle Mariners before signing a gargantuan $252 million deal with the Texas Rangers. Just three years into that 10-year contract, he was on his way to New York. Who is this well-paid individual?

**A** Shortstop/third baseman Alex Rodriguez. He is paid well because he plays well—usually. American League MVP in 2003 and again in 2005, A-Rod had 464 home runs by the end of the 2006 season. Still, he has been roundly criticized by some fans and sportswriters for a supposed lack of production in clutch situations. The jury is out on where he fits in the list of all-time greats.

**Q** It is not a pleasant memory for Yankees fans, so let's recall the 2004 ALCS loss to Boston as quickly as possible.

**A** New York won the first three games and then, to the surprise of virtually everyone in the universe, lost the next four. The Sox proceeded to sweep the St. Louis Cardinals in the World Series, finally absolving Harry Frazee for selling Babe Ruth to the Yanks more than 80 years earlier.

**Q** What key member of that Boston team then jumped to the Yankees?

**A** Johnny Damon, who had been with the Royals and A's prior to his four years in Boston. Damon hits for average, has lots of pop for a fairly small guy, and runs well. But he has one of the weakest arms among AL center fielders.

**Q** This former home run king waded into the steroids controversy in 2004, pointing the finger straight at Barry Bonds: "Henry Aaron never hit 50 home runs in a season, so you're going to tell me you're a greater hitter than Henry Aaron? ...I mean, come on now, there's no way you can outperform Aaron and Ruth and Mays at that level." Who was he?

**A** Reggie Jackson.

**Q** This 6' 10" lefty has won the Cy Young Award five times and pitched for the Montreal Expos, Seattle Mariners, Houston Astros, and Arizona Diamondbacks before coming to the Bronx in 2005. Name him.

**A** Randy Johnson. Originally a wild pitcher (in terms of walks and hit batsmen), he learned to pitch as well as throw and has since become one of the best in baseball today—although his career is nearing its end. As Johnson has gotten better, so has his paycheck; when he started with the Expos in 1989, he was making $70,000 per year and is now up to $16 million. At the time of this writing, the Diamondbacks want him back in Phoenix.

**Q** In June 2006, center fielder Bernie Williams played in his 2,000th game as a Yankee. Four others have done the same. Who are they?

**A** Mickey Mantle (2,401), Lou Gehrig (2,164), Yogi Berra (2,116), and Babe Ruth (2,084).

**Q** When was ground broken for the Yankees' new $1.2 billion stadium?

**A** August 16, 2006. The city and state will be contributing a fifth of that sum—a surprisingly small amount. It is being built on 22 acres at Macombs Dam Park and John Mullaly Park, adjacent to the old Yankee Stadium. No portion of the old stadium will remain. It is due to open in 2009, the same year as the New York Mets' new $610 million Citi Field in Queens.

**Q** What was the longest nine-inning game in major league history?

**A** It happened quite recently—August 18, 2006. The Yankees and Red Sox were playing the second game of a day–night doubleheader at Fenway Park. Starting at 8:07 p.m. and ending at 12:52 a.m., with a groundout by Boston's Wily Mo Pena, it lasted four hours and 45 minutes. This game, with 10 pitching changes, 437 pitches, and 34 hits, was a 14-11 New York victory.

**Q** What strange and tragic event happened soon after the Yanks' 2006 season ended in the playoffs?

**A** Pitcher Cory Lidle died when his small airplane crashed into a high-rise building in Manhattan.

**Q** Is there any doubt that the New York Yankees, owners of 26 championships, have the most glorious history in all of pro sports?

**A** No.

# MORE GREAT SPORT TITLES FROM TRAILS BOOKS

After They Were Packers, *Jerry Poling*

Always a Badger: The Pat Richter Story, *Vince Sweeney*

Baseball in Beertown: America's Pastime in Milwaukee, *Todd Mishler*

Badger Sports Trivia Teasers, *Jerry Minnich*

Before They Were the Packers: Green Bay's Town Team Days,
    *Denis J. Gullickson and Carl Hanson*

Chicago Bears Trivia Teasers, *Steve Johnson*

Cold Wars: 40+ Years of Packer-Viking Rivalry, *Todd Mishler*

Green Bay Packers Titletown Trivia Teasers, *Don Davenport*

Mean on Sunday: The Autobiography of Ray Nitschke, *Robert W. Wells*

Mudbaths and Bloodbaths: The Inside Story of the Bears-Packers Rivalry,
    *Gary D 'Amato and Cliff Christl*

New York Yankees Trivia Teasers, *Richard Pennington*

Packers By the Numbers: Jersey Numbers and the Players Who Wore Them,
    *John Maxymuk*

Vagabond Halfback: The Life and Times of Johnny Blood McNally,
    *Denis J. Gullickson*

*For a free catalog, phone, write, or visit us online.*

## Trails Books
*A Division of Big Earth Publishing*
923 Williamson Street, Madison, WI 53703
800.258.5830 · www.trailsbooks.com